World Politics

Titles in this series

Zygmunt Bauman, *Globalization: The Human Consequences*
Zygmunt Bauman, *Community: Seeking Safety in an Insecure World*
Norberto Bobbio, *Left and Right: The Significance of a Political Distinction*
Alex Callinicos, *Equality*
Diane Coyle, *Governing the World Economy*
Andrew Gamble, *Politics and Fate*
James Mayall, *World Politics: Progress and its Limits*
Ray Pahl, *On Friendship*

World Politics

Progress and its Limits

JAMES MAYALL

Polity

First published in 2000 by Polity Press in association with Blackwell Publishers Ltd

Editorial office:
Polity Press
65 Bridge Street
Cambridge CB2 1UR, UK

Marketing and production:
Blackwell Publishers Ltd
108 Cowley Road
Oxford OX4 1JF, UK

Published in the USA by
Blackwell Publishers Inc.
Commerce Place
350 Main Street
Malden, MA 02148, USA

ISBN 0-7456-2589-4
ISBN 0-7456-2590-8 (pbk)

A catalogue record for this book is available from the British Library.

Typeset in 10.5 on 12 pt Plantin
by SetSystems, Saffron Walden, Essex
Printed in Great Britain by T. J. International, Padstow, Cornwall

This book is printed on acid-free paper.

For my grandchildren

Contents

Acknowledgements   ix

Abbreviations   xi

Prologue   1

Part I: International Society

1   Origins and Structure   11

2   The Modernization of International Society   17

3   A New Solidarism?   26

Part II: Sovereignty

4   Nationalism   39

5   Self-determination   53

6   Reappraisal   67

Part III: Democracy

7   Historical Antecedents and Cultural
    Preconditions   81

8   International Law and the Instruments of
    Foreign Policy   94

9   Pluralism and Solidarism Revisited   106

Part IV: Intervention

10   Intervention in Liberal International Theory   123

11   Humanitarian Intervention in the 1990s   134

     Epilogue   149

     Notes   158

     Index   165

Acknowledgements

In writing even so short a book as this I have accumulated more debts than I can acknowledge here. Work on the book was begun while I was a member of the International Relations Department at the London School of Economics and Political Science, where successive generations of graduate students helped me to work out my approach to its subject matter. I am also particularly indebted to three LSE friends, Michael Donelan, Roger Holmes and the late Philip Windsor, with whom I have argued about the state of the world and its discontents for over thirty years. The book was finished at the Centre of International Studies in the University of Cambridge. There too my colleagues and students have been a constant source of stimulation and encouragement.

Chapters 4, 5, 6 and 9 are developed from an earlier version which appeared as 'Sovereignty, Nationalism and Self-determination' in *Political Studies*, 47/3 (special issue, 1999) © Political Studies Association. Earlier versions of chapters 7 and 8 appeared as 'Democracy and International Society' in *International Affairs*, 76/1 (January 2000), and of Chapters 10 and 11 as 'The Concept of Humanitarian Intervention Re-visited', in Albrecht Schnabel and Ramesh Thakur (eds), *Kosovo and the Challenge of Humanitarian Intervention: Selective Indignation,*

Collective Action and International Citizenship (Tokyo, United Nations University Press, 2000). I am grateful to the publishers for allowing me to reproduce passages from these essays.

Finally, I should like to thank Sidney Sussex College for welcoming me into the Fellowship in 1998, Albertina Cozzi for providing me with a refuge in Legnano, without which the final editing would never have been completed, and my wife, Avril, for providing me with constant support while refusing to take me too seriously. The defects of the book are mine alone.

Abbreviations

CMAG	Commonwealth Ministerial Action Group
ECOMOG	ECOWAS Monitoring Group
ECOWAS	Economic Community of West African States
EPLF	Eritrean Peoples' Liberation Front
GATT	General Agreement on Tariffs and Trade
IRA	Irish Republican Army
KLA	Kosovo Liberation Army
MFN	Most Favoured Nation
NATO	North Atlantic Treaty Organization
NGO	Non-Governmental Organization
OAU	Organization of African Unity
OSCE	Organization for Security and Co-operation in Europe
RPF	Rwandan Patriotic Front
SALT	Strategic Arms Limitation Treaty
UNHCR	United Nations High Commissioner for Refugees
UNITAF	United Nations International Task Force
UNO	United Nations Organization
UNOSOM	United Nations Operation in Somalia
USA	United States of America
USSR	Union of Socialist Soviet Republics
WTO	World Trade Organization

Prologue

It is fashionable to be sceptical about the significance of the new Millennium. The computer technicians, who now rule so many aspects of our lives, did their work with exemplary efficiency. Those who holed themselves up against the apocalypse need not have bothered. When the debris was cleared away after the celebrations – 20 tons of empty champagne bottles from the streets of London alone – the world looked much the same as it had the night before. Both the problems facing humanity, and its prospects, remained unchanged.

Yet the Millennium is as good a point as any from which to try to take stock of the state of world affairs. We could not give any intelligible account of either human problems or prospects, without reference to a calendar. In most cultures, people punctuate the year with celebrations at set times. In most cultures also, those who can manipulate the calendar, with the aid of the stars or a theory of numbers, command a huge following, presumably because we all secretly yearn for an insight into our destiny. Rulers, from Julius Caesar to Indira Gandhi and Ronald Reagan, have been as prone as the rest of us to employ soothsayers. But we also need the calendar for mundane reasons. We could no more organize our social and personal lives without it than we could do without roads to move about on or houses to live in. There is no need to apologize, therefore, for using the onset of the Millennium as a vantage point from which to look at the development of international society and its present aspirations and dis- contents.

Still, let us admit it, there is a problem with this vantage point. The idea of the Millennium is a profoundly ambiguous emblem for the modern world. On the one hand – in Western thought – it is associated with the politics of enthusiasm, the paradisal longings of people for a world born again, remade on principles of justice that have somehow got lost or been betrayed. On the other hand, the millennium is a trade mark of Western univer- salism, or hubris, depending on how one tells the story. It is true that, with the possible exception of Buddhism, all the major world religions have given rise to millenarian- like movements, that are inspired by the expectation of an ideal society. The same goes for Marxism, which until its demise many saw as a secular equivalent to a world religion. But the world itself is part of the Christian story. For all practical purposes the world is now organized – bound into a single world community even – by the Christian calendar.

The problem that the Millennium poses for the student of international relations is thus roughly as follows. If these relations are viewed from the perspective of compar- ative sociology, it is possible to discern patterns of behav- iour that cut across social and religious divisions. An analysis of these patterns will no doubt throw light on our common predicament, but at the price of draining life of its passion and drama. For that, there is no substitute for narrative. However, if our concern is with the story framed by the past two thousand years, then we must recognize that it is not of deep spiritual relevance to many of the world's peoples, and its longevity therefore cannot be

expected to resonate everywhere. Indeed, one aspect of
the story – the fact that it can be told so as to demonstrate
the superiority of Western civilization and values – seems
likely to fuel anti-Western millenarian-type movements.
One does not have to accept Professor Huntingdon's
thesis, that the Cold War will be followed by a clash of
civilizations, to predict that the energies of these movements are likely to be directed at challenging the struc-
tures and institutions of international society that were
developed during the era of Western expansion.[1] Indeed,
they are already doing so.

The politics of enthusiasm have their intellectual as well
as their grass-roots variants. The Millennium will also, no
doubt, be treated as a suitable case for deconstruction
within the academic community. The discovery that the
West and the world are not synonymous has already had
widespread intellectual as well as political consequences.
When the world was being integrated into a single economic and political system between the seventeenth and
nineteenth centuries, those who were responsible – the
philosophers, scientists and empire builders – were seldom
worried about the problems of cultural or any other kind
of relativism. At the start, they operated with an uncom-
plicated Mercantilist view of the world, in which there
were always winners and losers. On this view, the difference between trade and warfare was one of degree only.
Later, they advanced the view of a common human
rationality. In economics the rationalists sought to demonstrate that vice could be transformed into virtue through
the combination of the profit motive and open competition. In politics, they discovered that there were certain
human rights, which all persons possessed by virtue of
their humanity, and that these could be sharply differentiated from mere privileges.

These discoveries involved the substitution of a rationalist positive-sum world view, in place of the realist zero-sum form of universalism that had preceded it. Where it had once been accepted that one person's, or state's, gain was another's loss, according to the new doctrines, it was not necessary for both parties to gain equally for both to be better off. This view of the world offered an explanation of co-operation and laid the foundations for a secular ideology of social progress. It also created a conundrum. In a world made up of sovereign and equal human beings, endowed with the same fundamental rights, including the rights of individual and collective self-determination, how could one explain, let alone justify, the fact that a few powerful states had effectively enclosed the world and partitioned it amongst themselves. The fact that the two countries – Britain and France – whose competition sparked off the final act of enclosure, were the birthplaces of the industrial revolution and the Enlightenment respectively, and hence the progenitors of rationalist universalism rendered the conundrum even more complex.

It has never been resolved. Eventually, the recognition that the conundrum was insoluble played a part in the withdrawal of European imperial power after the two world wars. But, during the nineteenth and early twentieth centuries, evolutionary theory came to the aid of those who wished to defend Western dominion in terms of a doctrine of progress. In their view, European imperialism was the avatar of a future world civilization. Social Darwinism could not survive the obscene atrocities of the Second World War, at least as a respectable defence of cultural domination. But the almost immediate onset of the Cold War pushed the issue of alternative value systems, and the cultural relativism that their existence seemed to imply, to the margins of international political debate. It is only since 1989 that the lack of confidence in the cognitive foundations of our present economic, social and political arrangements has had a significant impact on the study of world politics.

Anti-foundationalism – the view that there is no solid basis of fact or truth underpinning our knowledge of the world – had invaded most of the human sciences much earlier, but, in this respect, as in others, the study of international politics was in a time warp, insulated from many intellectual currents by the dangers inherent in the nuclear stand-off. Nonetheless, its belated extension to the study of world politics seems peculiarly inappropriate, if only because the role of contingency in international politics has always ensured that, whatever convictions individual statesmen have held, they could not in practice assume that they were shared universally. Such foundations as were laid down in international relations were provisional, the result of laborious negotiation and always subject to revision. The basic principle of international law – *pacta sunt servanda* (treaties are binding) – was qualified by the codicil – *rebus sic stantibus* (conditions remaining the same).

These observations may suggest that international relations is a field wide open to postmodernist methods of analysis. The story can be told from so many different points of view that none can establish its unambiguous authority. Not only will it be claimed that these stories are of equal validity but there is no meta-narrative such as Christianity or Islam once provided. In other words, there is no general scheme, which can be relied on to impose a measure of coherence and unity on the diversity of human experience.

The argument of this book is that to follow this line of reasoning is both unduly perilous and unnecessary. Millennial enthusiasm is dangerous in politics because it can easily translate into intolerant exclusivity and/or aggressive xenophobia. Its intellectual equivalent – anything goes relativism – is dangerous for similar reasons: on the one hand, it separates a small band of *cognoscenti* from the rest of us; on the other, since what they know is that there is nothing worth knowing beyond subjective experience, they are potentially at the call of any political paymaster.

The idea that deconstructing the old world will necessarily lead to an improvement in the human condition is absurd. Why should it? If the answer is that it will only be possible to recreate a just world order once we have exposed the corruption of the economic and political system, this solution is hardly new. Many liberal and Marxist thinkers reached the same conclusion long ago. We are entitled to ask postmodernists (as much as liberals and socialists) about the principles on which the new order is to be constructed. To regard these as self-evident is to engage in the academic equivalent of the millennial fallacy. If, on the other hand, the answer is that there are neither principles nor identities, nor any rational ways of deciding between rival moral claims, that nothing is fixed and everything is in flux, how do we enter the argument at all? Indeed, what would be the point in doing so?

Postmodern relativism is unnecessary because it appears to assume that human institutions cannot survive – or at least lose their authority – once their cultural foundations have been exposed. It is no doubt true that their origins help to shape their subsequent history, but it does not follow that they will be subsequently proofed against modification by outside influences. Deep down all cultures are synthetic hybrids. The re-emergence in many countries of religious fundamentalism does not prove that trans-cultural debate, and mutual accommodation, is impossible, or that knowledge cannot be applied outside the specific milieu in which it was developed. Nor does the willingness of some believers to employ force, without regard to the precepts of international law, establish that the law merely applies within Western cultures. If cultures were hermetically sealed, the modern state could not have evolved, let alone the law.

'True on one side of the Pyrenees, false on the other': Pascal correctly identified the problem, not the solution. Since 1989 the problem of cultural and political diversity has re-surfaced in international life. It manifests itself in three closely related, and over-lapping, debates, which form the main focus of this book. These debates are about sovereignty, democracy and intervention. To be more precise, they are about the meaning and relevance of sovereignty – and its relationship to national identity and the principle of self-determination; about the claim that democracy should form the basis of the world order – with its corollary that democratization should be both the objective and the primary instrument of conflict resolution; and about the possibility of using outside force, not merely to deter aggression but to resolve civil conflicts – with the allied assumption that the justification for intervention should be humanitarian. Before turning to these themes, it may be helpful to revisit three questions that were addressed, either directly or by implication, in the writings of international society theorists, and which still provide the context within which they are conducted. First, what is international society? Second, who are its members? Third, what are its boundaries? In sketching an answer to these questions, I shall begin in each case by considering the traditional understanding before turning to such modifications as have been introduced, largely as a result of twentieth-century developments, and the new challenges that have emerged since the end of the Cold War.

Part I

International Society

1

Origins and Structure

The origins of international society are conventionally traced to mid-way through the second millennium of the Christian era. The diplomatic and legal practices that evolved following the European wars of religion enhanced the role of reason, interest and prudence in international politics and reduced the appeal to passion. This outcome of the Peace of Westphalia in 1648 was achieved by a negotiated consensus that the sovereign would henceforth be accepted as the final source of authority within his or her own domain. *Cuius regio eius religio* – roughly to each prince his own religion – was not a general edict of toleration, but it was the ancestor of the modern principle of non-intervention without which, arguably, a generalized system of international co-operation could not have developed. Religious faith was no longer considered a just cause of war, at least amongst Christian princes. In this sense, their mutual recognition of each others' sovereignty was a blow struck against the millennial impulse in human affairs.

On the basis of the sovereignty formula, other institutions of international society were refined, most notably the diplomatic profession, and the framework of international law. There were also three additional but contested aspects of the post-Westphalia system – the balance of power, the special role of the great powers and the place of war within the system.

If traditional international society was the immediate product of a peace treaty, from a longer-term perspective it was also the successor to the idea of a world empire. Behind this idea lay the long shadow of the Roman Empire, which in turn gave birth to the idea of a united Christendom. So long as these ideas persisted, they favoured the maintenance of a hierarchy of social and political relationships; and consequently also of differentiated, but overlapping, jurisdictions. Compared with the feudal order, the new international society of sovereign states was egalitarian, at least in theory. Since states, then as now, differed enormously in power and capabilities, the question arose as to what was to replace the concept of hierarchy as the ordering principle of inter-state relations.

The answer favoured by most theorists was the balance of power, a principle of such convenient plasticity that it could be advanced in defence of almost any conceivable policy.[1] It was primarily the great powers who were most involved in 'balance of power' politics, whether pursuing military superiority in their own rivalries, or the maintenance of a diplomatic equilibrium, where necessary at the expense of lesser states. It was only these powers, after all, which had the capacity to drag the whole system into general war. If this happened, the whole edifice would be threatened, including the extension of law from the municipal to the international arena. Great power, it was held, made for great responsibility. Consequently, the great powers were apt to claim for themselves the right to over-ride the law in the interest of order.

Thus, the principal of hierarchy was smuggled back into the organization of international relations, although established on the basis of power not right. Since there was no authority above the sovereigns, the only limitations on the right to go to war were those to which they had agreed themselves. In this way also, war, the devastating effects of which had led to the creation of the system in the first place, was institutionalized as the ultimate mechanism not merely for resolving conflicts of interests but for preserving international order.

This somewhat Panglossian account of international society can only be achieved by ignoring the intellectual debate that has always accompanied the attempt to map the relations among sovereign powers. Most writers have identified three available positions on the question of international co-operation and hence on the possibility of there being an international society. These go by different names, but may conveniently be identified as the positions of political realism, liberal rationalism and revolution.[2] For the realist, international society does not exist, and the only restraining element in the war of all against all is the principle of prudential self-preservation. For the rationalist, international society exists but it is a different kind of society from that of the state and should not be judged by the same criteria. For the revolutionary, international society will only exist to the extent that the brotherhood of mankind assimilates to the condition of domestic politics. In other words, international society is a state or should be one.

Both Wight and Bull, the most prominent of the modern theorists of international society, were careful to point out that their labels attached only to ideal types and that in practice the positions shade into one another along a continuum. They are not, therefore, strictly speaking, alternatives but coexist at any one time or place (and indeed in the mind of any one person), although it is fair to say that at some times, and in some places, one position may acquire the ascendancy, as realism did on both sides during the Cold War. For our purposes, the point to note is that there is a fundamental distinction – between pluralism and solidarism – that cuts through the three positions. By pluralism, I mean the view that states, like individuals, can and do have differing interests and values, and consequently that international society is limited to the creation of a framework that will allow them to coexist in relative harmony. It is the recognition by pluralists that it is possible for many, if not all, conflicting values to be accommodated within such a framework that distinguishes their position from indiscriminate relativism. By solidarism, I mean the view that humanity is one, and that the task of diplomacy is to translate this latent or immanent solidarity of interests and values into reality. For pluralists, one of the features that distinguishes international society from any other form of social organization is its procedural and hence non-developmental character. Solidarists, on the other hand, believe in the possibility of international constitutional reform and convergence. Only the most brutal and most dogmatic revolutionaries could fail to recognize the dynamic tension between these alternative forms of co-operation. During the twentieth century, there have been repeated attempts to find ways of resolving this tension at the international level.

Before turning to these efforts, let me briefly consider the second and third questions raised earlier – who are the members of international society and what are its boundaries? In the original formulation there was no doubt about the question of membership. International society was a society of sovereigns, not of people. There was room for dispute about who had a right to exercise sovereignty and under what circumstances it might be forfeited, but individual subjects had no international rights of their own. Faced with persecution in one country, they might find refuge in another – as the Jews did in England under Cromwell's Protectorate – but their ability to do so was a function of politics, not of law. *Cuius regio eius religio* meant what it said, that is, that it was for the ruler to determine the circumstances under which his subjects lived. In theory, domestic affairs had no place in international politics. In this sense international society was pluralist. Indeed, before the First World War there were few concessions made to solidarist principles.

The boundaries of the original international society were only slightly less inflexible than its membership. The Peace of Westphalia itself was concluded between the powers that had been directly involved in the Thirty Years War, but its principles were generally accepted within Europe. To the extent that in time non-European countries were accepted into the society of states, this was largely a function of geopolitics, and the fact that powerful political rivalries dictated alliances with the Ottoman Empire. No one seriously believed that their rulers had willingly bound themselves to what Burke referred to as the public law of Europe.

The restraints that theoretically operated within the European states-system did not govern relations between Europeans and other peoples. Indeed, as Western ascendancy was extended around the world, some authorities drew a distinction between the relations of civilized powers, that is, the members of international society, and those with barbarians and savages.[3] With the former – Muslim rulers or Indian princes – relations could be based on treaties but these were more provisional than treaties governing relations between civilized powers, and were mostly unequal in the sense that they often established un-reciprocated rights for Europeans living abroad. One example was the Capitulations, the system of British courts that operated in Egypt until the end of the nineteenth century. The Europeans recognized the existence of China and Japan, whose rulers had traditionally viewed

them as the barbarians, as powerful civilizations in their
own right. But in the early period, East–West relations
were insufficient in scope to challenge Western assumptions about the nature of international society, while later
on the Oriental powers were also forced into the expanded
system on European terms. Europeans defined non-liter-
ate cultures as savage. With regard to these peoples there
was no need to codify relations by treaty – although the
British and Dutch tended to do so – and under certain
circumstances there might even be a duty of conquest.

So long as Europe was ruled by dynasts the set of rules
they had established to govern their mutual relations left
them free to deal with outsiders more or less at will.
Philosophers might agonize about whether, beyond the
confines of European international society, there was a
community of mankind, or who was or was not covered
by the *ius gentium* (law of peoples), but most statesmen,
protected by their pluralist compact in Europe, felt free to
enclose and exploit the outside world. Traditional international society was thus seen as geographically restricted
and as an essentially fixed structure. The erosion of dynastic rule and the success of Western expansion called both
these aspects into question.

2

The Modernization of International Society

The attempt to graft a solidarist conception onto the original pluralist framework was largely a consequence of the nationalization of the state, first in Europe, and then, in reaction to European imperialism, elsewhere. It was also partly a consequence of the integrating impact of modern technology in relation to both security and economic welfare.

The ideal of popular sovereignty was established by the American and French revolutions. The key documents – the Declaration of Independence, and the Declaration of the Rights of Man and the Citizen – were national expressions of what were held to be universal rights. They were advanced within particular contexts, but self-consciously spoke for humanity, not merely for the inhabitants of the thirteen colonies and the citizens of France. A global society, based on the solidarist assumption of equal rights, was entailed in the ideas underlying these revolutions, even though their implications for international relations were only dimly perceived at the time. The defeat of Napoleon not only restored the *ancien régime*, but its international equivalent, the static conception of international society, that is confined geographically to Europe and in membership to sovereign governments. It was only after 1918 that the solidarist principle of national self-determination was transformed from being an aspiration of the democratic opposition into the legal basis of the new world order. As we shall see, this transformation was flawed by the practical impossibility of resolving the contradiction between the sovereignty of states and the self-determination of peoples. What nationalists wanted was a state of their own, once and for all, not a fluid situation in which they might periodically be required to cede territory to any dissatisfied minority that had missed out in the first wave of state-creation, and might subsequently claim the right of self-determination for itself. From this point of view, nineteenth-century nationalists were only selective solidarists – they wanted to join the club, not to change it. The same point can be made about the anti-colonial nationalists who achieved power after 1945.

Solidarism, nonetheless, influenced the 'constitution of international society' in two respects. The first concerned the use of force as an instrument of foreign policy; the second the legitimacy of empire. The enthusiasm with which the belligerents had greeted the outbreak of the First World War quickly turned to a deep revulsion; not only with war itself but with the diplomatic practices and secret treaties that had simultaneously propped up the balance of power as the corner-stone of the system, and ensured that it catastrophically broke down.

In 1795, the philosopher Immanuel Kant had published *Perpetual Peace*, a pamphlet in which he attempted to resolve the problem of war by drawing up a constitution for a pacific union of Republican states. In 1918, President Wilson of the United States attempted to achieve the same end by institutional means. His system of collective security failed because the world could not be made to correspond to the confederation of like-minded republics that Kant had envisaged. But although the idea that peace was indivisible remained implausible, Wilson established the unacceptability of armed aggression at the centre of all future debates about international order. When the Europeans counted their dead, few were prepared to view war as an institution of international society. On the contrary, from now on – and across the political spectrum – war would be regarded as the breakdown of that society. The United Nations Charter, like the Peace of Westphalia, did not seek to eliminate force from international relations, but unlike the earlier treaty the Charter did attempt to restrict its use to self-defence, or collectively agreed action to deter or prevent threats to international peace and security across international borders.

At first sight, the Great War not only left the victorious powers with their empires intact, but added to them the spoils of victory. Germany's colonies and the Levantine provinces of the Ottoman Empire were divided, primarily between Britain and France. Even Woodrow Wilson had not initially thought of the right of self-determination applying beyond the confines of the 'civilized' world. On the other hand, had he accepted the traditional idea that territorial title could be acquired by force, it would have contradicted the liberal ideology that underpinned the peace settlement. It would have meant that, as in the past, a right could be derived from a wrong. The new ideology appealed to the nascent nationalist movements of Asia and the Middle East, as much as those in Europe, precisely because it was couched in universalist, rather than in culturally specific terms. The presuppositions of those who held liberal views, in other words, were at odds with their own philosophy.

The solution to the problem was to create the League of Nations mandate system. Under it, the German colonies and Ottoman provinces were held in trust by the mandatory power, which was accountable to the League for the welfare of the subject populations. On the surface, the mandate system barely disturbed the European empires. Colonies had no separate legal personality of their own – although the British Dominions and the Government of India were partial exceptions to this rule – and were therefore not members of international society. The mandated territories were sometimes even folded into neighbouring colonies for administrative purposes, as the western part of the Cameroon was into Nigeria. A principle of international accountability on the margins of European empire was thus established, which inserted a time bomb beneath the concept of imperial legitimacy. Despite the different categories of mandates, the introduction of the underlying idea of accountability for them all signalled the growing, if reluctant, recognition that self-determination could not be confined to Europe.

The fuse on the time bomb was long. European governments had always been reluctant to accept, until forced to do so, that outsiders had equal rights. It was, for example, only at the second Hague Conference of 1907 that Asian and Latin American countries had been admitted to international society.[1] And it took at least until 1960 before the Western powers would admit that the imperial game was over; and that the implicitly racist categories of the mandate system could no longer be advanced as obstacles to entry. The imperial powers continued to denounce all external attempts to influence their colonial policies up to the point when they transferred power. On the other hand, they could not reasonably argue that those territories they held in trust, under the League mandate system and its successor the UN Trusteeship Council, should enjoy rights denied to the populations of neighbouring countries which they ruled on their own behalf.

Traditional international society was a minimalist association. It was concerned with the mutual recognition of sovereigns, with establishing their rights, including their right to form and change alliances, or to have their neutrality collectively guaranteed by their peers. But with little else. The enthusiasm of nationalist governments for this conception stemmed from its grounding in the legal principle of sovereignty which has always been more highly regarded by the weak and vulnerable than by the strong. New entrants to international society have always feared that they may lose their independence as the result of intervention, allegedly sanctioned on solidarist grounds, but in fact masking the economic and political interests of stronger states.

The economic and strategic integration of the world since the industrial revolution has also led to modification in the traditional conception of international society. This process amounts to a kind of technological solidarism, in that most countries are now heavily dependent on the outside world not just for the import of luxuries but for the basics of their existence and livelihood. In reaction to this interdependence there has been a tendency, throughout the twentieth century, to transform the quasi-constitutional order of international society into an enterprise association, that is, one that exists to pursue substantive goals of its own. The commitment of states to the pluralist framework still blocks the way to a fully fledged transnational society of this kind. However, the fact that most governments accept that people have positive as well as negative rights – as in the drafting of an international Covenant of Economic and Social Rights, or the continuing debate about the establishment of an international criminal court – illustrates the extent to which the international political thought has been penetrated by solidarist assumptions.

The case for a compromise between the principles of pluralism and solidarism is evident once we consider the origins of solidarist claims and the problems of implementation. The nationalization of the state was accompanied, almost everywhere, by the socialization of the nation. The claim that sovereignty was being exercised by the nation, and on its own behalf, led ineluctably to the view that the national economy had to be brought under national control and freed from foreign interference and exploitation. The underlying idea was the right of *all* people to manage their own affairs, but this implied the existence of an exclusive domain from which outsiders could be legitimately excluded.

The experience of the Great Depression and the Second World War led the major powers to conclude that economic welfare required the creation of institutions to lubricate the world economy with capital and credit, and police the liberalization of world trade – a kind of commercial equivalent of arms control. Even then, it was conceded that the government's duty to maintain full employment would, in a crisis, take priority over international obligations. The aim of the Bretton Woods institutions (the International Monetary Fund and the World Bank) and the General Agreement on Tariffs and Trade (GATT), was to achieve a rule-based diplomacy, but not at the expense of perceived national welfare. Not only was there no alternative source of authority to the state, there was no interest in seeking one. If economic order was to be maintained by a reciprocal exchange of most favoured nation (MFN) rights, there had to be national governments to make the exchange.

The same logic covered the establishment of regional and standing alliances in the absence of a credible system of collective security. On grounds of human solidarity, all governments had to refrain from aggressive war, but there had to be governments not only to do the refraining but to maintain a deterrent against potential aggressors. It applied also in the field of human rights, which were simultaneously regularly abused by governments, but could only be upheld by them.

This lopsided compromise between the pluralist world of self-interested states and the solidarist principles to which their governments were theoretically committed was challenged twice during the twentieth century. On each occasion the challenge was defeated. The first challenge was by the fascists and Nazis for whom the ideal of co-operation was anathema, whether it was the weak variety envisaged by the pluralist law of coexistence, or the stronger belief in a world constitutional order. Western international society could no longer unite against the barbarians, because they were already within the citadel. The compromise was challenged again and much more ambiguously during the Cold War. The East–West divide meant that for many purposes each side regarded the other as barbarian. As Martin Wight put it:

> Arguably, it was more reasonable in the years after 1945 to see world politics as divided into two international societies. That of western European origin, and the new communist one, their overlapping, as for example in the United Nations, being less important than their mutual exclusiveness, as in the non-recognition of Red China.[2]

The trouble with this view is that while it captures much of the strategic reality, it discounts the restraints on ideological disputes. These were obviously reinforced by the awesome prospects of nuclear war, but they were also entirely consistent with the Westphalia principles. There were, of course, enthusiasts on both sides who strained to embark upon a new holy war – either by rolling back the Soviet empire and engaging in all-out economic warfare or, by insisting that the east wind should prevail over the west, and putting in the tanks whenever it was necessary to insure against a change of direction.

In the end, the governments of the United States and the USSR repeatedly drew back from the brink. The negotiation of the Strategic Arms Limitation Treaty (SALT), before the end of the Vietnam war, indeed at the same time as the Americans were mining Haiphong harbour, provides a vivid illustration. It was entirely consistent with the traditional view of international society under which the great powers arrogated to themselves responsibility for international order.

The weaker states might grumble, but by and large, the strategic stalemate, coupled with the principles of restraint, suited the new entrants also. Having formerly outlawed the use of force as an instrument of foreign policy, traditional neutrality, guaranteed by potential belligerents, was no longer an option, although a few cases survived for particular reasons. But non-alignment secured their independence at less cost to their national pride, while allowing them to secure material advantages from both sides.

There was a final reason why international society, modified and modernized under the impact of nationalism and the doctrine of popular sovereignty, survived the Cold War. In the last analysis, the conflict was not about the rivalry of two civilizations, but about two possible ways of organizing industrial society. In this sense, it was indeed the equivalent of the sectarian conflicts of seventeenth-century Europe, requiring a broadly analogous solution. It is not obvious, however, that the analogy can be extended into the new millennium. The religious stand-off between sovereigns created sufficient stability to allow the industrial revolution to take hold, and eventually, however unevenly, to penetrate every corner of the globe. Over time it also led to the privatization of religion, at least in

the West. But there is now no equivalent need for a
secular stand-off, because the communist version of
modernity has withdrawn from the field. So, perhaps, we
have no further need of principles of ideological coexistence, and can replace international society by a global
community grounded on principles of human solidarity.

3

A New Solidarism?

The new solidarist vision is attractive but is fraught with perils. The fundamental problem is how to navigate without maps. There have been two kinds of proposals. The optimists believe that we should go with the flow. They see in the globalization of the world economy the retreat of the state from many of its traditional functions, and the emergence of a global civil society. Edward Hicks's Peaceable Kingdom will at last be achieved, although by liberating the people via the internet, rather than by the return to the garden of Eden envisaged by the painter. The pessimists foresee international anarchy finally overcoming the anarchical society of states, as the affluent lose their will to act and the weak states are first criminalized, and then collapse altogether. The politics of ethnic hatred and religious conflict will gradually undermine the precarious foundations on which international society rests.

Both versions are advanced by enthusiasts, who are united – or would be if they paused long enough to raise their eyes above the parapet – by the belief that the contemporary world order is fundamentally different from that in the Cold War period. It follows that what we most need to understand is the process of change. On this view, the study of international relations – indeed the task of social science in general – involves shooting at a constantly moving target. Even this metaphor is misleading because it implies that at least the target retains a recognizable shape, whereas it is in a constant state of flux and metamorphosis.

It is undeniable that, in many respects, the world at the start of the new millennium is markedly different from the world during the heyday of the eighteenth- and nine-teenth-century European states-system. The assumptions on which Vattel, or even Grotius, based their accounts of international life have been eroded, by making sovereignty popular, and then qualifying it by the assertion of individual rights. In the Grotian version it was still possible to regard international society as a kind of holding company for the community of mankind envisaged by the natural law. This possibility was swept away by the evolution of the state-system and the body of positive law that underpinned it. But it was not resurrected – as some contemporary cosmopolitans seem to assume – by the movement to entrench a raft of individual human rights beyond the reach of all authority. If individuals are sovereign, and rights ultimately trump obligations, what is left of the *community* of mankind?

Such evidence of conceptual evolution, and the intellectual and moral confusion to which it gives rise, should not blind us to the extraordinary continuities within all social relations, including those at the international level. Indeed, arguably, it is what stays the same, not what changes, that calls out for explanation. Like the poor, change is always with us. It is what withstands change, against the odds, that is truly remarkable. We know this intuitively from our own experience. No one who has lived past fifty can be unaware of the seismic shifts in the political landscape since 1945. The collapse of communism and the disintegration of the Soviet Union are only the most recent examples. But equally extraordinary is the demise of Britain, in scarcely more than a generation, from its position at the hub of the most extensive empire the world has ever known, to its present schizophrenic position on the edges of the European Union. Yet despite such buffeting, we still confidently believe that we are who we are. If we could not assume that our identities were proofed against time and circumstance, Lear-like, most of us would go mad.

The charge against traditional international theory is that it uses out-of-date maps to navigate in uncharted waters. Whether this is justified is up for debate. There is a respectable view that it is better to have inaccurate maps than none at all.[1] But let us, for the moment, accept that anachronism is to be avoided if possible. Is there a formulation that will establish the grounding of international society, throw light on its enduring qualities, and so help us to think more clearly about some of the recent challenges to which it has been subjected?

It is my contention that a formulation of this kind exists. In support of this claim we may call to the stand that most modern, yet sympathetic, of the classical philosophers. David Hume is surprisingly neglected by students of international society, yet with his insistence that our moral sensibility cannot finally outstrip our experience, he surely gets closer than most to the underlying character of international relations. Hume's three fundamental rules of justice seem better designed to survive into the new millennium, and to provide a compass by which to steer, than most of those currently on offer within the Academy. It will be helpful to quote him at some length. He begins his discussion of the Law of Nations by examining the problem that arises from treating a state as a person:

> . . . and indeed this assertion is so far just, that different nations, as well as private persons, require mutual assist-

ance.... But ... as they are very different in other
respects, no wonder they regulate themselves by different
maxims, and give rise to a new set of rules, which we call
the Law of Nations. Under this head we may comprise the
sacredness of the persons of ambassadors, the declaration
of war, the abstaining from poisoned arms, *with other duties
of that kind, which are evidently calculated for the commerce
that is peculiar to different societies.* (my italics)[2]

Thus far we have a classic defence of the pluralist conception of international society. Like individuals, states
cannot flourish in isolation. But, insofar as they are, so
to say, the containers of different societies with customs
and practices of their own, they must develop common
conventions and rules that will allow them to rub along
together. One might perhaps complain that not only is
Hume's language archaic – although it should be said
that in contrast to many contemporary texts its meaning
is as clear as crystal – but that his argument no longer
applies in a globalized world. However, the fact that war-
ring states these days seldom bother to declare war formally, pales into insignificance beside the enormous body
of law that allows them to coexist and co-operate without
having to align their peculiar cultural idiosyncrasies.
Before Articles 2.4 and 2.7 of the Charter are dismissed
as obstacles to human emancipation, we should recall the
creative and positive function that they perform in world
politics.

Hume is clear on this point. He continues:

But though these rules be super-added to the laws of
nature, the former do not entirely abolish the latter; and
one may safely affirm, that the three fundamental rules of
justice, the stability of possession, its transference by consent, and the performance of promises, are duties of
princes as well as of subjects. The same interest produces

the same effect in both cases. Where possession has no
stability, there must be perpetual war, where property is
not transferred by consent, there can be no commerce.
Where promises are not observed, there can be no leagues
nor alliances.[3]

From a contemporary vantage point, there is again the
whiff of anachronism. The Prince's responsibilities were
on a different scale from those of his subjects, but in the
final analysis he was as much a person, with his individual
interests and his own will, as any of his subjects. However,
the replacement of subjects by citizens complicates the
problem of treating the state as a person. An international
society of princes was a highly exclusive club with a precise
membership – only members of the princely class could
belong. When citizens aspire to rule the state on their own
behalf – and this is what the doctrine of popular sovereignty implies – they must develop procedures for express-
ing their corporate personality and resolving conflicts
between their individual interests and a putative national
interest.

The language of citizenship is universal and devoid of
cultural baggage – hence its appeal. One has to be a
citizen of somewhere – the idea of being a citizen of the
world is little more than a rhetorical flourish – so that the
concept is incapable in practice of standing alone. What
passes for the rights and obligations of citizenship in India
may approximate to the situation in Italy – and hence
provide a basis for comparison and even for the emergence
of transnational values – but they are unlikely ever to
overlap exactly. An international society of popular sovereigns, therefore, is likely to be both more porous and less
coherent than a club of princes. It contains within it
greater evolutionary potential than its predecessor but also
provides a more hospitable environment for inter-cultural

misunderstanding, mutual resentment and popular xenophobia.

If all this is conceded, it does little to weaken Hume's argument. Indeed, in some respects, it strengthens it. As the dividing line between the rights of sovereigns and the rights of individuals begins to blur, a rule of coexistence based on such minimal rules as can command general assent becomes more not less important. In other words, while both the membership and boundaries of international society may be increasingly contested, these struggles do not seriously challenge – indeed they are dependent on – the concept of international society itself. Nor could they challenge it, unless what was intended was either the revival of a world empire, or to do away with government altogether.

I shall consider in more detail the contested nature of the membership and boundaries of international society in later sections of this book. For the moment, let us review the question in the light of Hume's fundamental principles.

The question of membership can be broken down into three subordinate questions: How are new states to be created? Are non-state actors, including individuals, to be considered members of international society? What is the responsibility of the international community as a whole in answering these questions? To be consistent with Hume's minimal principles of justice for social life, it will in turn be necessary for the answers to these questions to be consistent with stability of possession, the principle of consent and credible guarantees.

In relation to the creation of states we face an immediate problem. As a glance at any historical atlas will reveal, stability of possession was not a traditional characteristic of international life. On the contrary, the realist view of international relations as a state of war reflected the widespread belief that they did not meet the minimum standards for social life. On the other hand, so long as territory changed hands on the battlefield, without, for the most part, having a devastating effect on social relations, it was also possible to regard war as an institution of an 'anarchical society'. Everything changed with the advent of popular sovereignty and the sacralization of territory that accompanied it.

Since no one could agree on what the right of self-determination meant, except in the context of European decolonization, this restrictive definition had the effect of providing the states with stability of possession. Great and small powers alike remained deeply opposed to territorial revision, as did the United Nations, not surprisingly since it reflected their views. Conversely, this solution was always resented by groups which simultaneously possessed a self-conscious political identity, occupied a territory that they regarded as ancestral, but were also stateless. In some cases, for example the Tamils of north-east Sri Lanka or the Kurds, divided between Iran, Iraq, Turkey and Russia, they had never been endowed with a dynastic or any other kind of state. Strictly speaking, therefore, they are on weak historical ground in arguing that they never agreed to the transfer of what they now regard as their rightful patrimony.

In this respect, states such as the Baltic republics, or even Ukraine, have a better case. The former enjoyed a brief period of independence prior to being forcibly incorporated in the Soviet Union in 1940, while Ukrainian nationalists can peer back over eight centuries to a period when their territory was not under the sway of Muscovy. But, since the issue is not about objective historical truth, as nationalists usually insist it is, but about perceived humiliation, insults and wrongs suffered by the group in the past, this comes close to being a distinction without a difference. Even if the state fractures for reasons that are largely independent of nationalist agitation, the resulting anarchy is likely to be experienced by its victims as a withdrawal of consent from the pre-existing government.

The belief that non-state actors have gained admission to international society derives from the empirical observation that businesses, inter-governmental and non-governmental organizations, transnational ideological and religious movements etc. increasingly influence both the way international relations are conducted and what happens. With the partial exception of the European Union, however, they cannot operate without the juridical cover provided by the sovereign state, acting either alone or in concert. As a general rule, such organizations do not challenge the minimal rules of social life, although their activities may inflame international tensions or foster co-operation depending on whether they are perceived as violating possession or facilitating free exchange. The activities of Hezbullah would presumably fall under the first head, those of the World Trade Organization (WTO), much more ambiguously, under the second.

The membership of individuals presents a different kind of problem because, since 1948, they have been acknowledged as right-holders on their own behalf. The underlying rationale of the Universal Declaration of Human Rights, its supporting Covenants and their various regional counterparts, holds that possession does not merely apply to territory or material goods, but in the first instance to persons. It follows that people must freely choose their own government and must be able to seek redress if their inalienable rights are violated. The unanswered question is from whom? Governments have signed these documents but they still refuse to hand over their policing to a higher authority that they themselves would have to create. The fact that the International

Criminal Court had to be emasculated before it could
gain acceptance by the majority of states, and that even
then the United States, China and several others refused
to sign, while by early 2000 only a handful of states had
ratified the Convention, indicates the difficulty. It is not
merely the inherent one of allowing individuals to challenge the authority of their own governments, or of
accepting that a special prosecutor may act on their behalf,
it also reveals that the boundary question is ultimately
ethical, rather than geographical. Without some agreement on what, or who, lies beyond the pale, the concept
of international society is empty of all content.

Who, then, if anyone, lies beyond the boundaries of
international society? It may be useful at this point to
recapitulate the answers provided within traditional international society, and in the same society under the impact
of modernization. In the first case, there was a boundary
– porous but still recognizable – between the states of
Europe and what their rulers perceived as being barbarian
peoples beyond Christendom. In the second period, the
universalist principles of the eighteenth-century revolutions gradually spread throughout the world. Once they
had done their subversive work, the rights of man and
citizen removed the barbarian option as a way of organizing international society. Notoriously, doing away with
the external boundary, the Other, out there, so to say,
went hand in hand with the rise of totalitarianism – the
Other in here and all around us. The new barbarians
could not be used as an organizing device because they
constituted an internal threat within international society
itself. After 1945 – and in reaction to the holocaust – an
attempt was made to draw an internal boundary which
both individuals and governments would cross at their
peril. The raft of inalienable human rights to which
governments put their name implied a democratic consti-

tution, without prescribing its precise form. Provided different national circumstances and cultures were protected by sovereignty, it was possible to reach consensus on the ends governments were supposed to serve, and the rights people were meant to enjoy.

The almost millenarian optimism that accompanied the end of the Cold War has put the compromise solution to the boundary problem in jeopardy. For the first time since 1918, solidarists scented the possibility of putting power to the service of law rather than the other way around. There was a predictable pluralist counter-attack. Much of the noise that surrounded the end-of-history debate smacked of special pleading on both sides. At the Vienna Conference on Human Rights in 1993, for example, those governments that championed Asian values were vigorously opposed by NGOs from their own countries which protested with equal virulence the case for a universal standard.

Nonetheless, there was a serious point buried within these polemical exchanges. It concerned the issue of responsibility – who has it and to do what? Traditional international society depended on self-help; governments were responsible for everything that happened within their borders, for the welfare of the inhabitants and defence against external attack. If they chose to pursue their interests by aggressive means beyond their own jurisdiction, they risked coming up against an alliance of opponents, who, following Hume's third principle, would have exchanged promises to come to each other's assistance. The attempt to abolish the use of force as an instrument of foreign policy was accompanied by a general breakdown of trust in the inter-war years. The subsequent vesting of responsibility for peace and security with the Security Council, in particular its permanent members, sought to restore credibility to the abolition, by allocating special responsibilities, rather than abandon it altogether.

The issue of responsibility is one that recurs repeatedly in this book. It seems to me that those who have attempted to promote the transformation of international society along solidarist lines have paid insufficient attention to two basic questions which must arise in any kind of purposive or enterprise association. Who is to pay the bill, and who ultimately must carry the can? This is not merely a failing of normative theorists; it extends to the highest levels of government. In their enthusiasm for an expanded international role in the security field, the permanent members of the Security Council spent much of the first half of the 1990s willing the end, but not being prepared to vote the means. Nor, as we shall see, was this style of politics confined to military affairs only. It is a style in which the rhetoric is sometimes aimed at a domestic audience, sometimes at an international one, but seldom follows a close analysis of either interests or consequences.

The start of a new Millennium is likely to provoke enthusiasts everywhere to indulge their fantasies in the hope of escaping from the unsatisfactory constraints of our present arrangements. It would be regrettable if governments followed suit. The old maps may be wearing thin in places, and no doubt these days they only provide the roughest of guides, but we would do well not to throw them overboard.

Part II

Sovereignty

4

Nationalism

These days, sovereignty often appears to be a beleaguered concept. Nonetheless, the formal order of international society continues to be provided, in the main, by the collectivity of sovereign states. Nationalist, and other, movements that challenge this order seldom attack the principle itself, since in the last analysis they mostly wish to acquire sovereignty for themselves. Their challenge is directed, instead, at the claims to legitimacy of those who exercise state authority. It is not states that nationalists wish to abolish, if necessary by force; it is existing, allegedly illegitimate, non-national states.

One of the consequences of the Cold War was to close down debate about the nature of international legitimacy. This observation may seem paradoxical, since the Cold War was, at one level, an ideological confrontation, each side claiming to represent the only just world order. Yet, so long as it persisted, a principle of strategic denial to the other side more often than not prevented any close examination of the democratic or popular credentials of existing governments. The Cold War notoriously made for strange ideological bedfellows.

It also cut down virtually all challenges to the state order that were mounted by stateless groups claiming their right of self-determination. Only Bangladesh fought its way to independence and international recognition; and even then only after the decisive intervention of India. We should be clear about what is and is not being said here. The Cold War did not prevent nationalist insurgencies, far from it, but from the vantage point of the major players in world politics, it rendered them largely invisible. Conversely its end, and the collapse of communism, not only led to the creation of more than twenty new states, but simultaneously reopened the debate about the meaning of the principle of self-determination, the nature and role of national identity in international politics, and the limits of sovereignty.

The debate opened in a spirit of high optimism that hid more than it revealed. The then United Nations Secretary-General, Boutros Boutros-Ghali, caught both the optimism and the confusion of the post-Cold War public mood in his *Agenda for Peace*, the document that was commissioned following the first ever Security Council Summit in January 1992. In his discussion of the new international context he made three statements that seemed to hint at a process of managed constitutional reform for international society. First, he insisted that the state must remain as the foundation stone, but that its authority was not absolute. 'Respect for its fundamental sovereignty and integrity are crucial to any common international progress. The time of absolute and exclusive sovereignty, however, has passed; its theory was never matched by reality.' Secondly, he argued that the United Nations had not closed its doors to new members, but that 'if every ethnic, religious or linguistic group claimed state-hood, there would be no limit to fragmentation, and peace, security and economic well-being for all would become ever more difficult to achieve'. Finally, he suggested that the way to resolve the rival claims of sovereignty and self-determination was through respect for human rights, particularly the rights of minorities, on the one hand, and democratization on the other. 'Respect for democratic principles at all levels of social existence is crucial: in communities, within states and within the community of states.'[1]

What, beyond these high-minded but somewhat bland pronouncements, can be said about the relationship between nationalism and the principles of sovereignty and self-determination? In answer to this question two arguments will be advanced in this chapter and the two that follow it. The first is that, paradoxically, there is not, and indeed cannot be, any final or determinant answer. This is because the meaning of the concepts themselves is contested, so that the relationship between them will shift over time, as political actors confront new opportunities and constraints and adjust their ideas accordingly. The second argument is that, despite this indeterminacy, a conventional understanding of the relationship between sovereignty, nationalism and self-determination emerged after 1945. Further, this understanding seems likely to prove more stable than some revisionists assume.

At the heart of this conventional interpretation was the belief that international society consisted of sovereign, that is, independent states; that they formed a society because they recognized each other's sovereignty and what this entailed, namely their territorial integrity and right to manage their domestic affairs without outside interference; and that consequently the right of self-determination referred only to colonies. This consequence, it should be noted, was historical and circumstantial: it was not a logical deduction from the principle of sovereignty.

This conventional interpretation remains largely intact, except that it is no longer plausible to argue that strategic necessity rules out territorial change, as it was during the Cold War. This may seem a small change, but it opens the floodgates. An illusion of stability has given way to an equally illusory sense of flux. Because the Cold War had so effectively frozen the political map, there was a tendency to assume that it had also interrupted the process of democratizing the international order according to the principle of national self-determination. The validity of this assumption is not self-evident – while self-determination can reasonably be held to imply self-government, the establishment of democracy cannot itself create a political identity which does not already exist. Nonetheless, the revival of the assumption that an international order that respected the right of self-determination would also entrench democracy certainly undermined the view that the national question had been finally resolved by the post-Second World War settlement.

Sovereignty is a much older principle in international politics than self-determination. The first aspect of the problem to consider, therefore, is what happened when the latter principal was injected into a world of pre-existing sovereign states. Traditional international society was largely composed of dynastic states. The patrimony of the rulers – and with it the borders of their states – could be changed as a result of the fortunes of war or the construction of dynastic alliances through marriage, and consequently also by the acquisition of title through inheritance. The members of international society were thus the sovereigns, not their subjects. This conception was challenged by the American and French revolutions, but the United States was only peripherally involved in international relations during its early years and, after the defeat of Napoleon in 1815, the old real-estate system was restored in Europe. It survived, dented but more or less intact, until the First World War.

Since 1919, international society has ostensibly been based on a principle of popular sovereignty, namely national self-determination. The collapse of the Habsburg, Hohenzollern, Romanov and Ottoman empires dealt a mortal blow to the dynastic principle. It was no longer possible to defend the state as a private possession of particular individuals or families. But if prescription was out, consent had to be in; ownership of the state, in other words, had to be transferred to the people. The difficulty in effecting this transfer arose because, in the last analysis, individuals alone can give or withhold consent. Yet individuals do not, and cannot, live alone. Which, therefore, are the appropriate collective selves, whose right to self-determination must be recognized as the basis of the new political order?

This question arose in the immediate aftermath of the First World War. It seemed to imply that statehood – and hence membership of international society – should be based on a democratic test of opinion. In practice, new states were created out of the debris of European dynastic empires, theoretically along national lines but with little attention to their democratic credentials. Similarly, after 1945 the European overseas empires and after 1989 the Soviet Union and the Yugoslav Federation broke up into their constituent parts. Since the implied principle of consent has not featured prominently in the three twentieth-century waves of state-creation, it is worth asking whether the questions, what is a nation, or who are a people, are theoretically answerable at all; or, on the contrary, can only be resolved pragmatically?

The rise to political prominence of the theory of self-determination was, in a sense, an accident. Empires had, after all, risen and fallen many times before in all parts of the world. At any other time in world history the revolt against the West would not have required theoretical support. At the time when the spectacular world-wide advance of European imperial power was halted, however, the arguments that were used to sound its retreat were those of Western political philosophy, all of which rested on their claims to universal validity.

Self-determination was a central concept in this tradition, independent of, and prior to, the rise of nationalism. From the late eighteenth century both contractarians and idealists had conceived of human freedom in terms of the political obligations of self-determining individuals. Rousseau made the crucial move by identifying the rational individual will with the General Will, so that obligations owed to the state were, in the final analysis, owed by the citizen to himself or herself. From whichever direction the argument was started, it finished up advancing the claims of nations to the allegiance of individuals. Thus, at one end of the spectrum, Mill held that for the concept of freedom to have any meaning at all, human beings had to be able to choose 'with which of the various collective bodies of human beings they choose to associate themselves'.[2] At the other, Hegel insisted that only the nation 'possessing in its own eyes and in the eyes of others, a universal and universally valid embodiment in laws' could form the basis of true, that is, ethical, as opposed to formal sovereignty.

From the point of view of international relations, the problem with all these reconciliations of political obligation with self-determination is that they take the identity of the nations themselves for granted. To be sure Hegel has criteria for distinguishing between true historical nations and groups which are, so to speak, suffering from arrested development, such as hunters and gatherers or pastoralists.[3] Mill did not explicitly rely on such evolutionary arguments, but his use of the distinction between civilized and barbarian peoples suggests that he too believed that a people's right to free institutions was evolved rather than natural in any *a priori* sense. But for neither writer was the identity of the group itself, as distinct from the issue of its rights, viewed as being problematic and therefore a suitable subject for theoretical analysis.

The theoretical problem emerges whenever it becomes necessary to decide which national claims to statehood should be recognized. The original Wilsonian solution to this problem was the plebescite. It failed, not merely because of the irreconcilable territorial claims in Central and Eastern Europe after the First World War, nor because the great powers had no intention of testing their legitimate title in their own possessions by this method, but also because it too regarded the identity question as self-evident. As Ivor Jennings famously put it in 1956, 'On the surface it seemed reasonable: let the people decide. It was in practice ridiculous because the people cannot decide until someone decides who are the people.'[4]

International society was forced, by the absence of an uncontentious definition of the nation, into settling the issue pragmatically, a step which was rendered doubly necessary once the right of all peoples to self-determination had been listed amongst the fundamental human rights in both the United Nations Charter and the Universal Declaration of Human Rights. This did not lead, however, to the obvious, and in my view correct, conclusion that no generally applicable and objective definition is available, but to a prolonged, if inconclusive, debate about the identity and origin of nations. The fact that the Cold War had virtually ruled out territorial change seems merely to have convinced the rival protagonists that it was the strategic stalemate that had removed the issue from the realm of practical politics, rather than its inherent insolubility.

Safely removed from any danger of influencing govern-

ments on such vital questions as the international recognition of insurgent or liberation movements, or
intervention in support of, or opposition to, such movements, the quest for the true identity of the nation was
transferred from the negotiating table to the academic
seminar. Nationalists, who were involved in liberation
movements, may have had their own views on the identity
question, and some of them indeed probably drew inspi-
ration from the ideas of particular social theorists, just as
nationalist governments used the school curriculum to
perpetuate national myths and construct national cultures
which both justified and ran congruently with state
boundaries. But in neither case could they appeal to an
agreed definition that would put their claims beyond
dispute.

Two broad theoretical answers have been advanced to
the question of national identity, although within each of
them there are a number of variations, some of which
overlap. Primordialists maintain that the national map of
the world was laid down a very long time ago, even if very
few these days cling to the belief that it accurately reflects
the natural world, which can therefore be assumed to have
remained essentially unaltered since the beginning of
human history. By contrast, modernists see the nation as
a recent invention, dating, except for a few somewhat
anomalous, or at least unexplained, cases, only from the
American and French revolutions.

For primordialist writers, assigning the right to self-
determination is, in principle, a soluble problem, however
difficult it may be in practice. Perhaps just because it is so
difficult, they do not often address the matter directly.
The recipe is deceptively simple. First find your ethnie.
This is done by identifying a group of people who share
one or more of a list of 'objective' characteristics (the 'one
or more' is normally added to accommodate Switzerland)

– a name, a common language, a homeland, in which they generally although not invariably reside, common symbols, a common myth of origin or ancestry and a sense of themselves as a people with a shared history of triumphs and disasters and, on the basis of these, shared hopes and aspirations.[5]

Next extract your ethnic group from wherever it has been washed up by the tide of history, be it within an empire or a multicultural state. Endow its members with a state, under a government of their own kind, and of which they are citizens rather than subjects. This last step will effect the transformation of the ethnic group into a nation and will equip the new state for entry into international society. Opinions seem to differ on cooking times: for some, providing the ethno-genesis has occurred at a distant point in the past, a nation-state can be expected to arise naturally on defrosting after the Cold War. Others, like Walker Connor, are more cautious, pointing out that the emergence of national self-consciousness from its ethnic base is a slow and uncertain process, about which it is difficult to generalize.[6] Much, it seems, depends on the oven.

Modernists hold that, far from nations rising up naturally from the ethnic subsoil in which they are rooted, they are created by nationalists, that is by those who subscribe to the political doctrine that nation and state should be congruent. Some nationalists may be able to adapt pre-existing ethnic myths and symbols for their own purposes, but they are also capable of inventing nations – Estonia is often used as an example – where prior to the age of nationalism, none existed.

The original modernist account of the nation was provided by those who attacked the *ancien régime* at the end of the eighteenth century. Their conception was broadly consistent with the liberal idea of self-determination as democratic self-government. The nation, in other words, was a civic association, not an ethnic one. The French insisted on the importance of French culture and language as defining elements of the French nation, but it is worth recalling that, for much of the nineteenth century, France was a host country for immigrants. The influx was not on the scale of immigration into the United States, but it was nonetheless significant. Official policy was certainly assimilationist, but it did not pay much attention to social or ethnic origins.

Academic modernists have paid almost as little attention to the international implications of their theories as the primordialists. For the most part, their interest is in the historical and sociological conditions that ushered in the nationalist era, rather than the justification offered for a state's entry into international society. Thus, for example, Gellner argued that a national culture was a necessary accompaniment of the transition from agricultural to modern society, largely because the division of labour on which industrialism depends, and the competition to which it leads, requires occupational mobility and therefore a literate and trainable labour force. Peasants, who mostly stay in one place, do not need to read and write in order to function and tend to regard whoever governs them with deep suspicion. Modern states, on the other hand, require educated citizens whose loyalty they can command. Another modernist author, Benedict Anderson, attempted to explain why citizens identify with the state by tracing the rise of the nation to the development of print capitalism; the profit motive requires a market of readers, which in turn puts a premium on the production of literary works in the vernacular and allows for an imagined community of people who do not know one another directly.

In neither of these two accounts does the demand for

self-determination feature prominently. Yet it is the modernists who point the way to the practical resolution of the self-determination problem. For Gellner, the crucial factor in determining a state's borders along national lines is the existence of a high culture, which is already widely diffused amongst the population at large, rather than being confined to the landed aristocracy and the clerisy, as it mostly was in traditional agrarian society. Gellner explained the political mapping of Europe during the nationalist era, by dividing the continent into time zones. Only along the Atlantic coast was there no great need to redraw political boundaries.

The point about the zone is that from the late Middle Ages, if not earlier, it was occupied by strong dynastic states, which roughly, even if only very roughly, correlated with cultural areas. This meant that when, with the coming of nationalism, political units had to adjust themselves to cultural boundaries, no very great changes other than a kind of *ex-post* ratification were required.

Consequently, with the exception of Ireland, 'the map of this part of Europe in the age of nationalism does not look so very different from what it had been in the age when dynasty, religion and local community had been the determinants of boundaries'.[7]

Elsewhere it was different. In the lands of the former Holy Roman Empire, two high cultures – Italian and German – had been codified since the Renaissance and Reformation respectively, although politically the area had long been fragmented. Political rather than cultural engineering was therefore required in the Italian and German speaking lands. It was carried out fairly successfully, from on top, by Piedmont and Prussia respectively. It was the area to the east that posed the greatest problem. In the Habsburg Empire and those parts of Europe under Ottoman rule which confronted it, there were many peasant communities which lacked both a high culture and a distinct polity.

Here both cultures and polities had to be created,

> an arduous task indeed. Nationalism began with ethnography, half descriptive half normative, a kind of salvage operation and cultural engineering combined. If the eventual units were to be compact and reasonably homogenous, more had to be done: many, many people had to be assimilated, or expelled or killed. All these methods were eventually employed in the course of implementing the nationalist political principle, and they continue to be in use.[8]

The same story might well have been repeated in the lands ruled by the Romanovs, had the Tsarist empire not, in effect, been taken over by the Bolsheviks. Apart from a hint of structural determinism, what is striking about Gellner's account is that, wherever possible, an existing provincial state was used as the basis for the creation of a nation-state. Thus the internal administrative boundaries of the former Habsburg and Ottoman empires were used to settle the boundaries to which the majority population was to succeed – Poland for the Poles, Albania for the Albanians and so on. The Bolshevik interlude in the erstwhile Romanov empire meant that it was not until after 1991 that the same principle was applied to the Soviet Socialist republics – the internal borders of Ukraine, Georgia and the rest becoming the new internationally recognized borders of the post-Soviet, and now independent, states.

A similar conclusion emerges from Anderson's analysis of non-European nationalisms.[9] Specifically, he confronts the failure of Bolivar's attempt to create a United States of Latin America. Why, given their access to a common literate high culture, did the South Americans not follow

where the United States had led? Essentially, his answer
is that the formative experience of South American nationalists took place within the provinces of the Spanish
Empire: for the Creoles – the Spanish-speaking but locally
born elites who aspired to independence – their 'career-
pilgrimages' not only defined the imagined community
but were constrained by the administrative boundaries
established by Spain. Only those born in Spain could
serve anywhere in the Empire; the locally born were
confined to their home province. The territorial units
existed before nationalism and represented a real rather
than a visionary prize for those who aspired to exercise
power.

With minor adjustments, Anderson's argument can be
applied to most non-European nationalisms. Certainly, it
seems to fit quite well in Africa, where the appeal of Pan-
Africanism was quickly subordinated to the territorial
principle after independence. Similarly, in India, following
the partition of 1947, any concessions that were made in
response to demands for regional and linguistic autonomy
– and many were – were never allowed to challenge the
territorial borders of the state inherited from the British
Raj.

Most modernist writers on nationalism adopt a broadly
realist approach to international relations, to the extent
that they consider them, which is not often. They seldom
address legal or normative questions. At the same time,
implicit in their arguments is the recognition that political
identity – like political boundaries – are contingent matters. This is the crucial point. The contingent cannot be
settled by rational argument, or by a democratic vote. For
political argument to take place, boundaries must be in
place, but they lie behind or beyond such argument all the
same. It was the reluctant recognition, born of bitter
experience between the wars, that this was indeed the case

Sovereignty

that led the international community to evolve an official interpretation on the principle of self-determination after 1945. Note that this interpretation, under which self-determination was viewed as a once-and-for-all act of decolonization, tied in time and space, was imposed by stealth – or at least incrementally – rather than by treaty or even by any openly acknowledged process of negotiation. Moreover, while the Cold War delayed any serious challenge to this interpretation, it was not responsible for its initial adoption.

5

Self-determination

When the drafters of the United Nations Charter, and the Universal Declaration of Human Rights, turned their attention to the right of self-determination, they referred to peoples rather than nations, presumably in an attempt to avoid the destructive confusion that had accompanied the reconstruction of Europe after 1918. The result was not a huge improvement. Finding objective criteria to define 'a people' is no easier than, indeed no different from, defining a nation, unless, that is, the right is assigned to pre-existing states or territorial units and the people, whoever they may be, are simply assumed to be identified with and represented by state governments.

Whether or not those who drew up these documents were already clear about what they were doing, the principle was in practice interpreted as applying – *ex-post facto* – to all existing states and to the overseas colonies of the European imperial powers. Despite a rearguard action by defenders of the imperial idea, it was not seriously advanced in relation to the Soviet Union's imperial legacy, on the eastern fringes of Europe, around the Baltic, in Central Asia and beyond.

Nor were most governments willing to insist on a democratic test of opinion before extending international recognition to states that underwent a revolution. The

United States attempted – for more than twenty years successfully – to blackball the People's Republic of China from the United Nations, but even Washington's closest allies were unimpressed by this attempt to force ideological conformity across international borders and in obvious defiance of Article 2.4 of the Charter. Irredentism got equally short shrift. Some colonial successor states consolidated their territory, around the edges of their inheritance, without suffering serious international consequences: thus India swallowed Goa, Indonesia, first West Irian and then East Timor. This proved much more contentious because by 1974, when the annexation occurred, the conventional interpretation had already emerged. Earlier, in 1951, China had absorbed Tibet, a decidedly premodern form of conquest which the outside world accepted because the country had never enjoyed formal sovereignty or international recognition. But in general during the Cold War there was widespread antipathy to opening up the domestic political arrangements of sovereign states to outside scrutiny, and no indication that the forceful pursuit of irredentist claims – outside the immediate context of European imperial withdrawal – would be tolerated.

Irredentist claims are seldom abandoned altogether, but the ambitions of governments which harboured them, such as Spain to Gibraltar, the Philippines to Sabah, Morocco to Mauritania, the Republic of Ireland to Ulster, the Argentine to the Falklands, and Taiwan to the Chinese mainland, faced formidable practical constraints. The irredentist states were prohibited under international law from using force as an instrument of foreign policy although the Spanish claim to Gibraltar was sympathetically viewed by African states on anti-colonial grounds. But, with this partial exception, it was impossible to generate diplomatic support within the General Assembly or other international organizations; and, above all, they were unable to obtain support for territorial change from either superpower.

The main challenge to the conventional interpretation of self-determination as de-colonization came from secessionists: these were, after all, precisely those who took the principle seriously, and who understandably drew the conclusion that, if self-determination was a fundamental human right, it should apply to them. Of the three Cold War secessionist crises, which spilled onto the world stage – Katanga, Biafra and Bangladesh – only the Biafran case was debated seriously in terms of the substantive meaning of self-determination. The reintegration of Katanga into the Congo was the price the United States was prepared to pay to marginalize Soviet influence within the United Nations peace-keeping operation. Academic analysts often explained the rebellion in East Bengal in terms of a theory of internal colonialism, but, as we have already noted, it was the Indian army which expelled Pakistan, not the Bangladeshis themselves.

Biafra's bid for independence collapsed because, unlike Bangladesh, Biafra failed to secure a powerful external patron who was prepared to defy the international consensus in favour of the territorial *status quo*. France came close, but in the end President de Gaulle indicated that he would be guided by African opinion. By 1969, four African states – Ivory Coast, Gabon, Tanzania and Zambia – had broken ranks and recognized the Biafran government. A number of others were rumoured to be sympathetic to its cause. At the annual Organization of African Unity (OAU) Summit in 1969, President Nyerere of Tanzania, who had himself proposed the 1964 OAU resolution, which committed African countries to accept the boundaries inherited at independence, circulated a memorandum to his fellow African heads of state.

He argued that, in this case, they should abandon the commitment. Nyerere's case was straightforward and compelling. Colonial borders, he suggested, had been accepted for practical reasons – to facilitate inter-state co-operation, to minimize opportunities for conflict and to release energies that could be better devoted to development and improving the lot of Africa's peoples. Nonetheless, the right of governments to rule rested on their ability to serve the population as a whole. When a government could no longer protect the lives of all of its citizens, and when a particular group believed itself to be threatened by genocide, it forfeited its legitimacy. In these circumstances, the same political considerations that had earlier led him to accept existing territorial arrangements could now (and in his view, should) be advanced in support of partition.[1]

This attempt, to establish internal standards of accountability and good government as relevant criteria for international recognition, failed. No surprise in that, perhaps. There was some truth in the jibe that, by 1969, the OAU had become little more than a trade union of rulers; few governments were genuinely answerable to their populations, and the life presidents and military dictators who attended its meetings had no interest in lowering their sovereign guard to accommodate international criticism. In most cases, internal opposition had been broken, or driven into exile. Also, in general, secessionists could neither appeal to international law nor dent the government's monopoly of the symbols of nationalism at the United Nations.

The lasting significance of Nyerere's failure, however, is that, unlike the failure of the United States to excommunicate communist China from international society, it had virtually nothing to do with the Cold War. The episode should give pause for thought to all those who may wish to argue that the end of the Cold War has created an opportunity to redraw the international map on the basis of 'genuine' self-determination.

The amazing sight of the communist regimes of Eastern Europe falling one after the other like a pack of cards in 1989, followed by the disintegration of the Soviet Union itself, may have temporarily led would-be revisionists to fantasize that an open season had been declared for secessionist self-determination. If so, the major players quickly disabused them. Even when, in March 1990, the Lithuanian parliament voted democratically to seek independence from the Soviet Union, Western governments withheld recognition and urged the nationalists to reach an accommodation with Moscow. Indeed, there is much truth in Misha Glenny's observation that, initially, the West 'understood self-determination to mean the right of east European countries to leave the Soviet bloc',[2] not the right of the Soviet republics to secede from the Union itself. The international community found it convenient to deal with the Soviet Union – once it had become clear that the centre would not hold – by treating it as though it were an empire. In this way its disintegration into its constituent parts could be understood as decolonization, thus leaving the conventional interpretation of self-determination intact. The main challenge to this hasty adjustment to international constitutional theory came on the one hand from Yugoslavia, whose communist government had avoided incorporation into the Soviet empire, and on the other from the Council of Europe and the European Union, both of which had established democratic criteria for membership.

In the event, despite sending contradictory signals to the competing nationalists in former Yugoslavia, the Europeans colluded in heading off the challenge to the conventional interpretation that they themselves had mounted. Thus, although the European Union appointed the Badinter Commission to establish whether democratic practices had been put in place that would justify recognition of the Yugoslav successor states, Western countries first discouraged the break-up of Yugoslavia altogether and then recognized it precipitously, paying only lip-service to democratic principles. At the same time, the outside world went to great lengths to ensure that the internal boundaries of former Yugoslavia and the successor states of the erstwhile Soviet Union – like the boundaries of their own former colonies – would define the international legal personality of the successor states. From this point of view, the Dayton Accords represent a victory for the conventional interpretation. So did the 1999 agreement under which NATO forced President Milosovic to withdraw the Yugoslav army from Kosovo. In neither case was secession recognized, let alone formally sanctioned. Admittedly, the Dayton Accords made provision for democratic elections as well as for territorial integrity. But whether, as a consequence, they will also mark the beginning of a new understanding of self-determination, in which acceptance of state borders is married to internal power-sharing, along confederal or consociational lines, remains to be seen. In other words, if democracy is to support rather than subvert the existing state, it will be necessary to entrench the rights of separate communities, by guaranteeing their internal autonomy, either on a territorial or on some other basis.

It is possible to construct a defence of national self-determination that is not linked to democratic values in the Western liberal sense. Miller, following Plamenatz, argues that there was nothing absurd in the belief of Europe's colonial peoples that they would have a greater sense of control over their own destinies if they were ruled by local oligarchies rather than alien imperialists.[3] But it is unusual. Self-determination is more often understood to mean the exercise of political freedom in which a people expresses its identity by choosing its own government. The people, in other words, are the final source of state legitimacy; hence the concept of popular sovereignty, which can only be separated from the democratic ideal by an appeal to tradition or some collectivist sleight of hand. Whether people will always opt for democracy given the chance to do so, and regardless of the consequences, is a different question. In any event, the democratic side won the Cold War. This victory ensured that claims for self-determination would henceforth have to be cast in democratic form. It did not, and indeed could not, resolve the underlying problem of political identity. Thus, to recapitulate: the right of all peoples to self-determination is a fundamental human right, but there is no secessionist right of self-determination. It follows that existing states are assumed to reflect the relevant political identities of the world's peoples. In this sense, territory has triumphed over the social composition of the population in determining both statehood and sovereignty. Political language, with its emphasis on democratic rights and legitimacy, conjures up an image of culturally homogeneous nation-states, whereas the reality is that most people live in multicultural state-nations, as they have done ever since the end of the age of empire.

This is hardly an elegant solution to the problem of political identity, but it is the only one presently available. Why are governments, including democratic governments, so deeply opposed to territorial revision? There is no single answer and, in any case, as we shall see, the obstacles to moving beyond the current position are mostly of a practical kind. Nonetheless, it may help to set the scene for our discussion of democracy, if we review three theoretical arguments that have been advanced in the past about the relationship of sovereignty, self-determination and secession.

First argument: that secession must be ruled out to avoid anarchy, and in the interests of public welfare. This was the position adopted by Abraham Lincoln during the American Civil War, and in a much diluted form it survives in Boutros Boutros-Ghali's *Agenda for Peace*. All citizens have the same fundamental rights, grounded in the constitution and protected by law. The only way the minority can become the majority, on this view, is by persuading a sufficient number of the majority to change their allegiance at the next election. Guaranteed rights of free speech and free association allow them, in principle, to compete on level terms with the government for the affections of the people.

The theory is attractive: there is no ground for holding that opposition will be regarded as treachery, and the government itself will be regularly held to account and will be changed following electoral defeat. The trouble is that at the end of the twentieth century, as in the middle of the nineteenth, it is not an accurate description of social reality in many parts of the world. In particular, as Harry Beran has pointed out, it cannot deal with societies that are structurally deeply divided.[4] The argument that Jinnah advanced on behalf of the Muslim League in the 1940s, was that Indian Muslims were a separate people, in a sense which would inevitably define and limit their political destiny. They could not see themselves as other than Muslims; and they could not hope to become the majority under any foreseeable circumstances. On the basis of this argument the British were eventually persuaded to partition the country.

Whether this was a wise, or indeed a necessary, decision will no doubt continue to be debated amongst historians and nationalists in both India and Pakistan. The relevant point here is that, until power was transferred at midnight on 15 August 1947, the British remained in control and were, therefore, in a position to take the decision. International society has no such authority to settle conflicts in societies where people insist on identifying themselves in ethnic or communal terms rather than as citizens. Nor has it shown any interest in acquiring it; nor indeed in partition as an instrument of international conflict resolution.

The refusal to countenance secession under any circumstances has had predictably gruesome results. After the Croatian Declaration of Independence in 1991, the government wooed international recognition by passing legislation to protect Serb rights. The trouble was that Serbs were not reassured and continued to resist rule from Zagreb. A blind eye had to be turned towards the ethnic cleansing of the Krajina before Croatia would accept the American-brokered settlement in Bosnia. Similarly, when in 1994 the Rwandan Patriotic Front (RPF) began to close in on Kigali, the Hutu-dominated government of Rwanda launched a genocide rather than surrender power. In such cases, Lincoln's splendidly civic argument fails to address not merely the aspirations but, much more importantly, the fears of the people on both sides of the conflict.

The most obvious objection to allowing a secessionist right of self-determination is that partition invariably creates new minorities, groups stranded on one side of the line or the other, for whom the *status quo ante* was better than the new dispensation. Nationalists may say that you can't make an omelette without breaking eggs, but that is of little comfort to the eggs. Beran's rational libertarian solution to this dilemma was to make the right of secession dependent on a principle of regressive self-determination. In other words the secession will be recognized if, and only if, the new government is prepared to extend the same right to minorities within its jurisdiction. That minority would then have to deal with its own population in the same way, and so on until the resulting territorial arrangements left no groups stranded and dissatisfied.

There are, in turn, two objections to this ingenious proposal. First, in practical terms, it is extremely difficult to believe that governments anywhere would take it seriously, even though its operation would probably act to keep the lid on the Pandora's box of claims and counter-claims which they so fear. It would, for example, make the secession of Quebec from Canada impossible unless the Parti Quebecois was prepared to grant the same right to the 'first nations' which have already declared their opposition. Establishing such a right in advance of any particular claim would be viewed as an open invitation to dissident groups to destabilize the government; would involve endless litigation about the division of assets; and would require a level of rational debate about competing claims, the absence of which is normally the hallmark of secessionist conflicts.

Secondly, even if these problems could be overcome, there is a theoretical objection to the proposal. Once the process has started, those who preferred the *status quo ante*, because it allowed them to maintain multiple identities – for example, to be both a Quebecer and a Canadian – or merely to occupy a private space within a multi-ethnic state, will find themselves forced to declare for one group or another, as the Yugoslavs were forced to do after 1991. Under cover of rational argument, one form of contingency will have been substituted for another. The defence would have to be that it would make the international commitment to democracy more credible. Perhaps. Whether the world would be a more peaceful or a more tolerant place is more doubtful.

Second argument: that democracy will be subverted and political freedom destroyed, where two or more powerful national groups compete through the ballot box to capture the state. This is the instrumental, as distinct from rights-based, defence of partition advanced by Mill in *Representative Government*. Written in the 1860s, it can be read as an almost uncanny prediction of what happened in Yugoslavia in the early 1990s. Mill's argument is implicitly historicist: a non-national or civic national democracy will only emerge if peoples of different nationality have grown accustomed to living together – and being governed under a single authority – prior to the era of both nationalism and democracy. However, if national self-consciousness and a desire for 'free institutions' emerge together, the absence of an overarching political culture will ensure that democracy will act as a source of conflict rather than of legitimacy.

The merit of Mill's argument is its concern with practical outcomes rather than collective rights in any abstract sense. His primary concern is how to protect human freedom; his advocacy of partition under certain circumstances is directed to the same end, not the conservation of particular national cultures or forms of life, as ends in themselves. For those committed to the latter objectives, it is his indifference to minorities which are not sufficiently numerous to strike at the democratic foundations of the state that most weakens his argument's appeal. Except in this limiting case, Mill was as opposed to secession as Lincoln, and his assimilationist assumption that minority discontent could be overcome by education, while benign in intention, and possibly true in some cases and over the very long term, has been falsified by events in many parts of the world.

Something of use can still be salvaged from Mill's brief but percipient observations about nationalism and democracy. Because there is no satisfactory *a priori* criterion for settling state boundaries, international society has settled for investing those that actually exist with an absolute status which belies their contingent origins. It also belies the fact that, in those cases where boundaries do change, the new map quickly becomes as sacred, and consequently as unnegotiable, as the old. When we contemplate the levels of destruction and human suffering that have frequently resulted from the defence of these boundaries, it might be prudent for statesmen, scholars and lawyers to adopt a more open-minded approach to territoriality than they have customarily done. Despite the minority and identity problems that invariably follow from secession, a second-best solution may sometimes be preferable to no solution at all. If this is not conceded, a bleaker and more traditional option remains.

Third argument: that while the existence of a nation is a prerequisite for democracy, nations will come into being, in the future, as in the past, only through a process of struggle and self-assertion against other forms of imposed imperial sovereignty. This argument, which was advanced in the aftermath of the Cold War, by Enoch Powell, a British politician, rests on a compelling but not necessarily ethnic logic. The essence of representative democracy, Powell argued, is majority rule. No matter how consociational the constitutional arrangements, there will always be some party or interest that is left out of the ruling coalition. So what is it that persuades the minority to put up with rule by the majority? Lincoln had suggested that it was the opportunity to change the government by swinging public opinion behind the opposition. But why should they be prepared to wait, particularly if the odds on success are long and there is a better chance of influencing events by taking the law into their own hands?

Powell's answer was that the minority will only put up with majority rule, if there is some overarching community sentiment which is stronger than the conflicts of ideological, economic or political interest that customarily divide people on a daily basis.

It is not clear that a community of this kind can be engineered, at least from outside. But we know that most, if not all, well established nation-states develop democratic institutions only after a prolonged period of power struggles and feuding at home and abroad. Even the United States had to fight a civil war to prove to themselves that they were one people and not two. Collective amnesia, as Renan famously remarked, is a defining characteristic of most nations, as much as shared memories and traditions. Whether it is true that behind every great fortune there is a great crime, it is difficult to think of a great nation (or even a small one for that matter) that does not rest on great cruelties and/or injustices – in the past.

The difficulty posed by this argument is only too apparent: on the one hand, as an account of how the democratic world came into being and maintains itself, it is plausible; on the other, insofar as it condemns us to live – indeed to define ourselves – by the sword, it is morally repellent. Moreover, it is not merely liberals, but governments of all ideological persuasions, which have accepted the legal prohibition on the use of force except in self-defence. The twentieth-century world wars, on this view, were fought, at least partly, to replace the rule of the sword with that of the constitution, internationally as well as nationally. This process was interrupted by the Cold War, which marginalized the role of the United Nations in maintaining international order. Between 1947 and 1989, the patronage and protection of the superpowers was frequently extended to tyrannical governments of both left and right.

But there is no evidence to suggest that the popular hunger for self-government that erupted after 1989 was an aberration. If, as I have argued, it is impossible to devise rational rules for redrawing the political map to accommodate the aspirations of all politically self-conscious groups, it remains to ask whether there is an alternative way of interpreting self-determination within international society.

6

Reappraisal

It is not surprising that, in unknown terrain, governments seem determined not only to proceed with extreme caution but even refuse to acknowledge that change is either necessary or desirable. And it is true that, from one point of view, not much has changed. The conventional interpretation of self-determination as decolonization referred to international recognition, not always to the situation on the ground. Thus, for example, over the past fifty years, Chad and the Lebanon were sometimes effectively partitioned, even though, at the international level, their sovereignty and territorial integrity were maintained. Many Asian, African, and Latin American countries were also never pacified in the sense implied by the theory of internal sovereignty; that is, they were in a constant state of armed rebellion with whole regions where the writ of the central government did not run, sometimes for years on end. Yet in virtually no case were rebel forces able to challenge the legitimacy of the government at the international level.

So far, the post-Cold War expansion of international society has been accommodated by treating the disintegration of the Soviet Union and the collapse of communism as a form of decolonization. Armenia and Azerbaijan have been recognized as independent states, but Armenia's military occupation of Ngorno Karabach has not been recognized any more than was Israel's occupation of the Golan Heights after the 1967 war. In both cases occupation was accepted as a strategic reality by those involved, but from an international and legal perspective these occupations were regarded as anomalies and remained on the political agenda as outstanding problems awaiting resolution.

Similarly, the international community followed Russia in recognizing the sovereignty and independence of the former Soviet Socialist Republics – as a generation earlier it had followed Britain and France in recognizing their transfer of power to nationalist governments in the former colonies. The analogy can be pressed further. During British and French decolonization, the activities of Corsican separatists or the provisional IRA were never viewed as part of the anti-colonial movement. The British and French governments occupied permanent seats on the Security Council, and so were in a strong position to resist any attempt to internationalize these 'internal' demands for self-determination. But, amongst anti-colonialists, there was no sustained attempt to argue that the 1960 United Nations' Declaration on Decolonization (General Assembly Resolution 1514) should apply in such cases. Apart from other considerations, to have pressed such a claim would have implied that the principle of *uti possidetis juris* (the law of holding what you currently possess) would have been undermined at the very point when vigorous efforts were being made to establish it as an un-negotiable international norm in the context of decolonization.

In the post-Cold War world, the Russians were not immunized quite so effectively from international criticism of their handling of successive crises in Chechnya. But such criticism stopped well short of any international pressure on Moscow to concede the Chechynan right to an independent state. In sociological and empirical terms a strong case could be made that Chechnya had a better claim to independence than, say, Belarus, but as an autonomous region in the Russian Federation, it did not have the pre-existing legal credentials to fit easily into the conventional interpretation. Recognition would, therefore, not merely have been resisted by Russia, which like Britain and France occupies a permanent seat on the Security Council, it would have been regarded by the international community generally as setting a dangerous precedent.

Three other considerations may help to explain the underlying reasons for the reluctance of governments to reopen the question of self-determination. Each illustrates a different aspect of the theoretical problem.

The first is the obvious difficulty in reconciling the principle of self-determination, however conceived, with the deliberate use of force to change an international boundary. Historically, this was one of the principal ways that the political map had been redrawn, but after 1945 the UN Charter rejected the right of conquest. The new constraint was, so to speak, the flip side of the principle of *uti possidetis*. It was all right for the governments of both established states and successor regimes to accept this principle, because inheritance could be assumed to have originated prior to the emergence of democratic self-consciousness or the awareness of universal human rights. It is a different matter altogether to try and put the clock back and to create a new right – namely possession – by what has come to be accepted as a wrong – namely an act of territorial aggression.

It was precisely because the attempt to transform the political landscape in Bosnia by force challenged the normative framework of international society at its most vulnerable point that the major powers acted as they did. The uneasy peace that was eventually brokered at Dayton,

Ohio, in 1995, and which has been kept precariously in place by NATO peace-keeping forces, showed the extraordinary lengths to which the major Western states were prepared to go to maintain the principle of territorial integrity. It was impossible to return all territory that had been conquered, ethnically cleansed, and then repopulated in the preceding four years, to their original owners. Indeed it remains doubtful whether even the loose confederal arrangement that was negotiated could survive without the continued presence of international forces. So long as they remain, however, the future of Bosnia's political identity and territorial integrity will be maintained and may, in time, constitute a new reality. If this is the outcome, the international community will have successfully asserted its right to determine the internal constitutional arrangements, as well as the external boundaries, of states that seek international recognition. Whatever the final outcome, with regard to territorial self-determination both the Dayton Accords and the Kosovo settlement reinforced, rather than modified, the conventional interpretation.

A second aspect of the theoretical problem is how to prevent a successful bid for international recognition spilling over into, or otherwise destabilizing, the wider region in which the claimant's state is embedded. The doctrine of *uti possidetis* was formulated in nineteenth-century Latin America as a means of putting an end to a destructive and potentially unending cycle of irredentist conflicts. Since 1945 the doctrine has been promoted in particular by the African states whose governments feared that conceding the legitimacy of any secession would open a Pandora's box of claims, from which none of them could escape. The doctrine was therefore built into the foundations of the OAU at an early stage. Neither Morocco, which until 1969 claimed Mauritania and continues to claim large sections of the western Sahara, nor Somalia which claimed the Ogaden, Djibouti and the north-eastern province of Kenya have ever been able to breach the solid wall of diplomatic opposition to their claim.

Nor, at least openly, were the Eritreans able to obtain diplomatic support for their secession from Ethiopia, to which they had been attached in 1952, with scant regard to their wishes.[1] That they were eventually successful has less to do with the emergence of new criteria for recognizing the legitimacy of self-determination claims than with the power vacuum following the Soviet Union's abandonment of its client regime in Addis Ababa in 1991. The predominantly Tigrean government that moved into this vacuum was itself allied to, and heavily dependent on, the Eritrean Peoples' Liberation Front (EPLF). Since its defeat of its rival in the 1970s, the EPLF had kept the Ethiopian army pinned down in Eritrea and made the country ungovernable, at least after dark. The new Ethiopian government was not in a position either morally or practically to resist Eritrean independence. Even so, other African governments continued to be nervous in case a precedent was being set which would lead to the unravelling of the OAU's territorial settlement.

They need not have worried. The Eritreans – like the East Timorese – had always argued, without success but with some justice, that by demanding an independent state of their own they were upholding, not attacking, the conventional interpretation of self-determination as decolonization. Unlike Ethiopia, whose government had itself taken part in the nineteenth-century scramble for Africa, Eritrea has been colonized by Italy and then administered by Britain in the Second World War, only being attached to Ethiopia by the General Assembly when the great powers could not decide amongst themselves about what to do with the territory after the war.[2] On this view,

Eritrean independence has merely brought the situation into line with the OAU orthodoxy that only ex-colonies can claim statehood. There are very few other potential claimants that can meet this criterion. One such is the self-proclaimed Republic of Somaliland, which comprises the former British protectorate, but Eritrea has been no more sympathetic to its claims than other African governments.

Eritrea was finally admitted to the United Nations and OAU in 1993 after 99.8 per cent of the population had voted for independence from Ethiopia in a referendum which was heavily observed by international organizations. As the referendum was a condition of recognition, it may be cited as evidence of a new democratic standard for entry into international society. Maybe. It is possible, perhaps more likely, that the referendum should be regarded as a rite of passage, which tells us little about the future trajectory of the new state. The Eritrean plebiscite not only failed to give minorities in Eritrea rights of self-determination but banned political parties for five years, after which they are to be permitted providing they are not based on ethnic, linguistic or religious differences. After so massive a vote of confidence in the national plebiscite, one might wonder why such restrictions were considered necessary. Within five years the new state was locked in a ferocious territorial war with Ethiopia, hardly an encouraging prospect for future liberalization.

Until 1999, the nationalist movement in East Timor, which like the EPLF could plausibly claim to have the conventional interpretation on its side, made little headway in its effort to reverse its forced incorporation into Indonesia. Despite a sustained campaign at the United Nations, support from Portugal and widespread international sympathy, possession remained nine-tenths of the law. The government in Jakarta was not dependent on an outside patron in the way that Mengistu's government in Addis Ababa was dependent on the Soviet Union: in these circumstances *uti possidetis* has a more traditional meaning. The situation changed dramatically after the financial crisis that led to the fall of President Suharto. I shall consider the wider implications of his successor's agreement to a UN-administered plebescite in part IV of this book. But we may note here that international support for East Timor has not been followed by similar support for the Acehnese and other breakaway groups. Unlike East Timor, the rest of the Indonesian archipelago had fallen under the administration of the Dutch East Indies. It therefore meets the conventional criterion for national self-determination, understood as a once-and-for-all event at the time of decolonization.

The third problematic aspect of self-determination is how the implied principle of self-selection can be reconciled with rules of entry to international society. The insistence in the Charter on territorial integrity, as a logical entailment of the principle of sovereignty, commits the United Nations against unilateral secession, not against secession *per se*. There has never been any objection, in principle, to the breakup of existing states providing separation is negotiated, as it was between Norway and Sweden in 1905, the Irish Free State and the United Kingdom in 1921, Malaysia and Singapore in 1965, and Slovakia and the Czech Republic in 1993. Nonetheless, while such negotiation may open a pathway to international recognition (this was presumably what Boutros Boutros-Ghali had in mind in suggesting that the UN had not closed its doors to new members), even democratic governments are reluctant to invite peaceful territorial challenges to their authority.

Where such challenges appear imminent – as in Canada from Quebec – the authorities are more likely to invoke the conventional interpretation in an attempt to head it off at the pass. Thus, in 1996, the Canadian government referred two questions to the Supreme Court of Canada. These were respectively, 'whether there is anything in Canada's constitution or in international law that would give the National Assembly, legislature or government of Quebec the right to declare Quebec's independence unilaterally', and, in the event of a conflict between the Canadian constitution and international law on these questions, which would take precedence.[3] The Supreme Court endorsed the view of the two international experts consulted by the federal government. These experts concluded that 'outside the colonial context, there is no recognition of a right to unilateral secession based on a majority vote of the population of a sub-division or territory, whether or not that population constitutes one or more "peoples" in the ordinary sense of that word.' It is true that both experts hedged their bets by suggesting that 'there may be developments in the principle of self-determination according to which not only colonialism but also flagrant violations of human rights or undemocratic regimes could lead to a right of unilateral secession', but they were firmly of the view that these putative developments are not relevant to Quebec.

In the meantime, the recent history of many countries that have been racked by civil conflict suggests that the concepts of sovereignty and self-determination were as contested at the end of the twentieth century as they were at the beginning. Yet, the view persists that because it cannot be shown to have an unambiguous meaning in contemporary politics, the concept of sovereignty itself is an anachronism. Let us conclude, therefore, by returning to this fashionable claim that sovereignty is no longer relevant for the analysis of world politics. The charge is an old one, reflecting, in the final analysis, the tension between authority and power. The two concepts are clearly not synonymous, but whether it is possible to possess one without the other, and if so, for how long, is a moot point.

There are strong and weak versions of the attack on sovereignty. Those who reject the concept altogether claim that the state has forfeited its traditional and central role in international politics, becoming just one actor – and not often the most important – amongst many. In the weak version it is argued, more plausibly, that the state has surrendered some of its attributes – for example, its ownership and control of a national economy – but has retained others – for example, its responsibility for the welfare of its citizens. On this view, the state does not lose its sovereignty, it merely has to adjust to a rapidly changing international environment, if it is to perform its essential functions.

The state has not withered away but its competence has certainly narrowed, in particular in the face of the globalization of the economy. To this extent it may be that the shift from the emphasis on empirical to juridical statehood within international society now has a wider application than when Robert Jackson developed it in relation to post-colonial states.[4]

The contrast that he drew was between the meaning of sovereignty within the European state-system and its interpretation within the UNO after 1945. Originally, it had been assumed that a sovereign state was one in which those ruled could make their writ run throughout the territory over which they claimed jurisdiction. When states recognized one another, and entered into diplomatic relations, or even went to war, it was on account of this reality. Where political communities lacked this level of competence, they could not expect to survive, or be accepted into international society. They were likely to fall prey to the imperial ambitions of neighbours or more distant powers, or be regarded by them as the inhabitants of *terra nullius* (roughly speaking no man's land). They might be protected from absorption by geographical remoteness or a lack of valuable resources, but they had no intrinsic right to independence. In 1960, however, empire was proscribed as a legitimate political form, and shortly thereafter the European powers gave up any attempt to make economic viability a condition of independence. It was sufficient to have been a colony with borders drawn by the imperial powers. Many of the new states lacked the capacity to sustain themselves by their own efforts, either politically or economically. They became, in effect, wards of the United Nations. Yet the international legal order was still invoked to buttress the authority of the state – its juridical right to independence – arguably to compensate for its dwindling capacity, but not to replace it.

The new world of virtual sovereignty that seems to have emerged since the end of the Cold War differs from that of juridical sovereignty insofar as the requirement of empirical independence is increasingly being dropped for states generally and not just for post-colonial states. To this extent the critics of sovereignty may be right. Where they are wrong is to assume that its use serves no real purpose. Just as the first iron-builders adapted the existing and familiar technology – building bridges with iron rather than wooden mortise and tenon joints – so the global marketplace is being constructed by adapting rather than abandoning familiar concepts. Indeed, as territorial borders become more easily penetrated by trans-national economic flows and other forces, territory itself appears paradoxically to have become if anything more rather than less sacred. This is primarily, no doubt, because it is held to belong to the people. It is difficult to imagine a present-day equivalent to the Louisiana purchase or the deal by which Alaska was transferred to American sovereignty. Modern government, to paraphrase Burke, has been given over to 'sophists, calculators and economists', but the territory over which they preside – and the popular emotions that are identified with it – remain stubbornly beyond their control. In this context, pre-existing title is a major asset, if not in every case a prerequisite, for entry into international society.

Here again there seems to be as much continuity as change. In the 1970s, India allowed Bhutan to enter the United Nations, despite retaining *un droit de regard* over its foreign policy, in recognition of historic title. The same concession was not extended to Sikkim, which had been more fully integrated into British India. In the early 1990s, as the Soviet empire disintegrated into its constituent parts, two West European micro-states – Andorra and San Marino – whose international personality had previously been expressed largely through their postage stamps, slipped into the United Nations almost unnoticed.

In the post-Cold War world there are both economic and political reasons for making such adjustments in the membership of international society. Globalization has reduced the plausibility of List's ideal of national political economy,[5] but not the appeal of national political autonomy. It is noticeable, for example, that amongst the resurgent nationalist parties in Eastern Europe and the former Soviet Union, there are few advocates of national protection, let alone autarky. Rather, self-determination is more likely to be interpreted as the right to compete in the deregulated market for inward investment. In contrast, the European Union has created a regulatory framework for its members, which requires them to negotiate as a single unit in international trade negotiations, and in other ways limits their ability to go it alone. At the same time, throughout Western Europe, there has been a resurgence of nationalism in stateless regions that nonetheless have a historic political identity. Those who speak for such regions, from Catalonia to Scotland, often see positive advantages to being directly represented in Brussels rather than, or in addition to, state capitals. By the same token, the existence of the European Union may allow national governments to be more flexible and accommodating in dealing with internal demands for devolution or decentralization in the name of self-determination.

There are obvious dangers in assuming that Western Europe is a model for other parts of the world, where the state has evolved from different antecedent conditions and along different trajectories. On the other hand if, as Alan Millwood has argued,[6] the European community should be understood not as a proto-European superstate but as a mechanism created by the states themselves to ensure their survival, there is no reason why sovereign authorities in other regions and continents should not prove equally resourceful and inventive.

Part III

Democracy

7

Historical Antecedents and Cultural Preconditions

Since the end of the Cold War the virtues of democracy have been championed on all sides. In his *Agenda for Peace*, the then Secretary-General of the United Nations, Boutros Boutros-Ghali, insisted that 'respect for democratic principles at all levels of social existence is crucial: in communities, within states, and within the community of states.'[1] At much the same time, the Council of Europe and the European Union were indicating to the westward-looking ex-Communist states, that they would have to establish their democratic credentials before being allowed to join the club. The Commonwealth drew up the Harare Declaration in 1991, its members pledging themselves 'to work with renewed vigour to promote the fundamental democratic values of the Organisation.' Four years later they went further, establishing a standing committee of foreign ministers, the Commonwealth Ministerial Action Group (CMAG) 'to deal with serious or persistent violations' of the Harare principles.[2]

For its part, the United States, now in lonely eminence as the one remaining superpower, enthusiastically endorsed – indeed some might say fashioned – the mood of democratic optimism. Anthony Lake, President Clinton's first National Security adviser, announced that 'the successor to a doctrine of containment must be a strategy of enlargement'. This strategy, he continued, 'is based on a belief that our most fundamental interests lie in the consolidation of democratic and market reform'.[3] It had not always been so. George Kennan, the author of the strategy of containment, had frequently deplored the American tendency to see his or her own political system as a model for mankind. In the mid-1970s, when President Jimmy Carter had briefly flirted with an ethical foreign policy, Kennan wrote that 'misgovernment, in the sense of the rise to power of the most determined, decisive and often brutal natures, has been the common condition of most of mankind for centuries ... It is going to remain that condition for long into the future, no matter how valiantly Americans insist on tilting against the windmills.' Better, he argued, that they should concentrate their energies where there were possibilities of useful and effective action. 'These, as it happens, are ones that have little relation to the cause of democracy as such.'[4]

How much has really changed in the quarter of a century that separates these two sets of views about the nature and possibilities of international relations? Can the internal constitution of states be determined by international society and can international society itself be democratized? These are not questions to which we can expect to find agreed answers if only because, as we have already observed, the nature of international society is contested. Few would dispute Boutros-Ghali's claim that the promotion of democracy is an end in itself, a condition which, ideally, is part of the birthright of every human being; but it is debatable whether, as he also argued, the promotion of democracy should be 'part of the responsibility of the United Nations to maintain international peace and security'. The purpose of the next two chapters is to examine how and why democracy has come to occupy such a prominent position in contemporary international relations, and to sketch some of the opportunities but also the problems that have arisen as a result.

The story of international society can be told in one of two ways. We have already encountered the standard version but it may be helpful to briefly recapitulate the argument here. It traces its emergence to the peace treaties that followed the European wars of religion in the mid-seventeenth century. These treaties established a kind of proto-constitutional order for a society of sovereigns under the formula *cuius regio eius religio*. The establishment of this society was followed by the development and refinement of its major institutions – international law, diplomacy and, more contentiously, the three ordering mechanisms, the balance of power, the special rights and obligations of the great powers, and War.[5]

At its inception the borders of international society were roughly congruent with those of Christendom, but over the next two hundred years the society became global, exported from Europe under the impress of strategic, geopolitical, economic and ideological competition. Not all the member states were invariably governed by hereditary, let alone absolute, monarchies – indeed, two of its founding members, Switzerland and the Netherlands, were decentralized republics – but many were. They established the standard. International society was overwhelmingly princely, always aristocratic. In any case, the formula under which the princes recognized each other's independence precluded making the internal political arrangements of states a legitimate concern of their neighbours. Conquest could change the map, and when it did so, as in any real-estate transaction, the new owners could make whatever changes in the ideological furnishings of their property as they saw fit. But, in that international co-operation between sovereigns was dependent upon

non-interference in each other's internal affairs, the underlying value of the society was coexistence. It is in this
sense that international society can be described as pluralist: it did not require agreement on substantive values
other than sovereignty. Nor did it involve the pursuit of
common projects.

The revised version was the product of the European
Enlightenment and the rise of nationalism. On the one
side it developed from the rationalist attack on prescriptive
right and rule; on the other, from the romantic counter-
attack, the assertion that the boundaries of state and
nation should coincide. I have argued elsewhere that,
despite successive shocks to the international system deliv-
ered by these forces, the society of states survived with its
essential structure intact.[6] Partly this was because, after
the defeat of Napoleon, the old regime was restored; partly
because what we now see as global processes – demo-
graphic change, industrialization, mass education, class
conflict etc. – were for a time successfully internalized or
exported through migration to the Americas. Primarily,
however, it was a consequence of basing the system on
the territorial state.

It was not until 1919 that the principle of national self-
determination was finally accepted as the theoretical foundation of a new world order. But the result of making
sovereignty popular was to sacralize territory. It could no
longer change hands as the result of victory in battle, or
be purchased as bride money or, in the New World,
outright. Tom Mboya, the first Foreign Minister of
Kenya, informed the Somali population that they could
exercise their right of self-determination anytime. All they
had to do was walk across the border into Somalia. Until
forced by NATO to withdraw his forces in June 1999,
Slobodan Milosovic's attitude to Kosovo was enforced
more brutally, but was essentially the same. A society of

popular sovereigns turned out to be more jealous of their prerogatives than their princely forebears.

So, international society survived. However, the Enlightenment and nationalism had two long-term consequences that have had a bearing on the role of democracy in international relations. The first was to introduce the idea of progress: legal and diplomatic arrangements that states agreed on to facilitate their relations, and overcome conflicts of interest, were no longer viewed, so to say, out of time, but as a way station on the route to a final destination. The goal of political life, abroad as well as at home, was to be human emancipation. The idea of universal human rights that had been inscribed in the American Declaration of Independence and the French Declaration of the Rights of Man and the Citizen held out this possibility for mankind as a whole, not just for Americans and Frenchmen.

The idea that politics should have a solidarist goal, and that this should be reflected in the evolution of international society, was resisted passionately, both in theory and on the battlefield. But, the seductive appeal of the progressive idea, harking back to the sovereignty of good over evil, has never been displaced altogether. Hope, it seems, springs eternal. Moreover, since the eighteenth century, the object of hope has not been salvation in another world but the improvement of the one we live in. Indeed, it is one of the great ironies of contemporary history that after each of the two world wars – as after the Cold War – there have been energetic, if sadly short-lived, attempts to refashion international society along progressive lines. In each case, the focus was different; after 1918 to redraw the map according to democratic and nationalist principles; after 1945 to transform the state, by national and international means, into an engine for the production of economic welfare and development; after 1989, to reinterpret sovereignty in a way which would prevent it from being used to protect tyrants who preyed on their own people. Each of these attempts was driven by democratic arguments.

The second consequence of the Enlightenment and the rise of nationalism was to entrench not democracy itself, but democratic values, as the standard of legitimacy within international society. The majority of states were no more democratic than they had been in the past, but after 1919 democratic values were increasingly accepted as a kind of ideological equivalent to the coin of the realm. Democracy was legal tender everywhere, even if circumstances prevented it from being minted in most parts of the world.

By democratic values, I do not just mean open representative government, but also the fundamental human freedoms of association, speech and belief, and the rule of law by which these goods are guaranteed to all members of the population, whether they are supporters of the government or not. The international status of this attractive, although not widely available, package has risen erratically over the past two hundred years.

There are several reasons for this development. One is the ability of power to generate demonstration effects. In the nineteenth century, it was not just the British Navy which underwrote the Pax Britannica, while sterling lubricated its commerce; British ideas of constitutional government and justice carried enormous prestige. Of course, the exercise of power also produced resentment, but this was more often directed at the powerful state than at the values, which seemed to accompany its success. The same holds for the United States since 1945. The institutional infrastructure – starting with the United Nations itself – is heavily influenced by the American model of federal democracy: the General Assembly is a kind of House of Representatives, while the Security Council is a kind of

Senate and Presidency rolled into one. Each body oper-
ates by a free exchange of views leading to a vote, but
each also has different responsibilities and represents different interests, in the one case the equality of sovereign
states, in the other the political hierarchy of power. The
Presidency is collective, and a veto of any one of its
permanent members is theoretically sufficient to stop
international action dead in its tracks.

Another reason for the popularity of democracy is the
role it played in decolonization. Britain and France, which
were primarily responsible for the final enclosure of the
world within a single diplomatic and political system, were
not merely national, as opposed to dynastic, imperial
powers, they were also democracies. They justified their
rule by various evolutionary and/or civilizing doctrines,
but in time these began to look threadbare as anti-colonial
nationalists first internalized Western democratic values,
and then turned them against the metropolitan governments, with devastating effect.

France and Britain eventually handed over to Presidents
and Prime Ministers, Assemblies and Parliaments that
were in the first instance modelled on metropolitan practice. No matter that in many cases democracy did not
long outlast the transfer of power. It had been grafted on
late by an essentially authoritarian colonial regime, and
authoritarianism was often quick to reassert itself. But
democratic politics had played its part in undermining the
legitimacy of imperial government, not least because it
allowed the emergence of a liberal anti-colonial 'fifth
column' within the French and British political establish-
ments. It is no accident that it was non-democratic Portugal that was the last of the European imperial powers to
decolonize.

The final reason for its popularity was that democracy
was regarded as a necessary ingredient of modernity.

Admittedly, until very recently, there were many that believed that modernity was best pursued by holding some democratic values in reserve. Few anti-colonial nationalists were serious Marxists, but many saw in democratic centralism and the command economy a doctrine which, from their point of view, had multiple virtues. It was anti-capitalist, important in countries where the government presided over a society that lacked an indigenous capitalist class. It was anti-Western, a bonus for regimes which were often uncomfortably aware of the continuing power of the West in their affairs. And it offered an alternative, non-Western route to the Promised Land of economic affluence to which all governments aspired. As Professor Hansen pointed out, even so liberal a leader as Jawaharlal Nehru pursued throughout his political life a dream that it would be possible to combine a Western polity with a Soviet-style economy.[7]

Paradoxically, the rival sponsorship of the two alternative versions of democratic theory by the two superpowers ensured that international society would continue to work as a minimalist and pluralist association, in circumstances which were roughly analogous to those that had led to the establishment of the European states-system in the seventeenth century. Both theories had their own versions of what human solidarity across international borders ideally required, but in neither case had the implications of these requirements for international relations been systematically addressed. The sudden collapse of communism internationalized liberal democracy almost overnight. The circumstances could hardly have been less propitious.

How should we measure the impact of democracy and democratization on international society over the past ten years? Before turning to this question we need to confront another which was of no great concern in the original version of international society, nor except at the margin in the revised version, but is unavoidable if plural democracy is to be regarded as potentially a world-wide system of government. Are there cultural preconditions that must be met before democratic values can become embedded in both national and international politics?

The question did not arise in traditional international society because what went on within a prince's jurisdiction was essentially his own affair. Indeed, it is plausible to assume that one reason why the institution of diplomacy evolved was to provide a core of specialists who could understand foreign cultures sufficiently well to minimize the risk of conflict, and/or develop a ritualized way of doing business between countries that did not, therefore, have to understand one another. The question only arose marginally within mid-twentieth-century international society because the geo-strategic stand-off between the rival camps largely confined the battle for hearts and minds to propaganda. And in any case both camps of cold warriors conducted the debate in a remorselessly Western, not to say fundamentalist, idiom.

Does the question arise now? Not if one assumes that the technological and economic pressures of globalization have created an homogenized MacWorld full of computerized nomads, all empowered with abstract rights but empty of significant cultural difference. One does not need to invoke Freud's narcissism of minor differences, to know that this is not, in fact, the world we inhabit.

So the question is important, however difficult it is to answer. My own inclination is to suggest that what matters is not so much the idiosyncrasies of particular cultures – the clothes we wear, the food we eat or even the God or gods that some of us still worship – that creates the major obstacle to universalizing democratic government. The essential problem lies in the different forms of life still to be found amongst human societies.

This point is, perhaps, best illustrated by example. Between 1803 and 1806 President Jefferson sent Captain Merriweather Lewis to explore upper Louisiana. Lewis was to find a navigable water route to the Pacific. He did not find it, because no such route existed, but he did make the journey, providing along the way the first ethnographic account of the peoples who lived along the Missouri and across the Rockies on the banks of the Columbia River.

It was American policy to bring peace amongst the various Indian nations, in order to incorporate them into the American trading system, and break the British monopoly of the northern fur trade. Like the British policy of substituting legitimate trade for the slave trade in nineteenth-century Africa, this policy had little to do with democracy as such, although Jefferson apparently hoped that the Indians – unlike the slave population from Africa – could in time be civilized and fully integrated into the American system.

Lewis set about his task of peacemaking amongst the nations of Missouri during the first winter he spent at the Mandan villages in today's North Dakota. He explained the advantages that would flow from a general peace, but his arguments came up against an insurmountable cultural obstacle. This arose, not from a failure to understand democratic reasoning but from its own logic. The old men agreed with him but only because they 'had already gathered their harvest of laurels, and having forcibly felt in many instances some of those inconveniences attending a state of war'. But a young warrior then put a question that Lewis admits he could not answer. '[He] asked me if they were in a state of peace with all their neighbours what the Nation would do for chiefs.' The present chiefs, he continued 'were now old and must shortly die and the Nation could not exist without chiefs'.[8] The Hidatsa Indians, like most of their neighbours, lacked a hereditary ruling class. All men were armed, and leadership was exercised by approbation and example, not by right. In an egalitarian and nomadic society, direct democracy of this kind is not merely the norm, it is a prerequisite for survival.

It may reasonably be objected that this is an extreme example, that the subsequent American policy of 'ethnic cleansing' made the United States safe for representative democracy, and that there are few parts of the world as untouched by modern ideas as the Missouri River in the early 1800s. But the point is not about the survival of indigenous peoples, although, as we shall see, this has emerged as an important issue in the discussion of the international protection of human rights. It is rather to illustrate how different forms of life, such as nomadism, pastoralism, settled agriculture, or industrialism, structure the range of options. We know, for example, that in at least one contemporary case, Somalia, the attempt to graft the institutions of a Weberian state onto a pastoral nomadic society with no pre-existing tradition of central-ized government went disastrously wrong. Southern Somalia is now effectively stateless, and while many peo-ple suffer as a result, devising an electoral system which would command the consent of all Somali clans, while addressing their actual fears and aspirations, has so far eluded Somali and non-Somali alike.

It may still be objected that this is another extreme example, an anomalous and marginalized country in what is economically and politically the most marginal of con-tinents. But if respect for democratic values is to be not merely the ideological coin of the realm, but the entry ticket into international society, it will have to embrace the indigent underclass of states as well as those with medals on their chests and national museums full of the looted art of the world's major civilizations. However it is dressed up, that is what democracy means. In any case, while Somalia may be an anomalous case, in that nomads are notoriously difficult to turn into national citizens, once it is conceded that ways of life limit the forms of government which will be viable under different circumstances, it is difficult to avoid the conclusion that there are many other countries where the preconditions for representative democracy are simply missing.

Ernest Gellner summed up the problem with his usual incisiveness. 'While democracy is not inherent in human nature, it does have some kind of affinity with the condition in which we find ourselves.'[9] He meant those of us who live in industrial societies, 'committed to growth and hence to occupational instability', and who consequently cannot rely on a rigid social hierarchy to enforce order. But, at the other end of the spectrum, he could equally have been referring to the Missouri Indians or the modern Somali. The problem lies not with fully industrialized societies, or with the few surviving pastoral or hunter-gatherer societies. It lies with all those that occupy neither of these positions.

It does not follow from these observations that a commitment to democratic values should have no place in international relations, merely that the democratization of international society, if feasible at all, will necessarily involve a great deal of constitutional ingenuity on the one hand, and hypocrisy on the other. To quote Gellner again, 'Theorists of democracy who operate in the abstract without reference to concrete social conditions, end up with a vindication of democracy as a general ideal, but are then obliged to concede that in many societies the ideal is not realisable.'[10]

Hypocrisy is the price that vice pays to virtue. Whether it is a price worth paying will depend on whether the attempt to establish democracy internationally saves human lives, reduces the level of arbitrary oppression, and provides at least some people with opportunities they would not have otherwise enjoyed, or on the contrary, leads to high levels of oppression and social conflict. This is a question of judgement not principle. The answer will vary from case to case, and even then, will be necessarily indeterminate. It remains to ask how well the institutions of international society have dealt with this challenge.

8

International Law and the Instruments of Foreign Policy

At first sight, international law, the bedrock institution on which the idea of an international society stands or falls, is not well suited to the discriminatory flexibility that seems to be called for if democratic values are to be seriously pursued at the international level. To begin with, this was not a major problem since the scope of international law was quite deliberately restricted to what could be agreed between, so to say, consenting sovereigns acting in private. Indeed, according to Professor James Crawford, classical international law was 'deeply undemocratic, or at least capable of operating' in six deeply undemocratic ways. In summary, these are: first, the comprehensive power of the executive to agree to and apply international laws over the heads of the people and often without their knowledge; second, the absence of democratic control over the international obligations to which a state is bound; third, the executive has 'virtually exclusive' control of the availability of international remedies; fourth, the principle of non-intervention protects 'even non-democratic regimes in relation to action taken to preserve their own power against their own people'; fifth, the principle of self-determination is not allowed to alter territorial boundaries; and sixth, a government can bind its successors far into the future.[1]

If the final test of international democracy is taken to be the translation of the society of states into a community of mankind, no doubt overcoming the first three of these undemocratic legacies will be crucial. Unless rulers, both individually and collectively, are answerable not merely to their national populations but to people everywhere, and unless individuals can indict their rulers when their fundamental rights are abused, it could be argued that international law will act to restrain the process of democratization rather than to encourage it. Given the diversity of cultures, constitutions and social conditions, moulding them into a single legal regime would not only be a Herculean task, it would consign the discussion to the realm of utopian speculation.

It is not surprising therefore, that it is in respect to the fourth and fifth undemocratic aspects of international law that the pressure for change has been most sustained since the end of the Cold War. To recap, these are that 'the principle of non-intervention extends to protect even non-democratic regimes'; and that 'the principle of self-determination is not allowed to modify established territorial boundaries'. These are the most obvious pressure points because they expose the tension between state power and the doctrine of popular sovereignty.

For the layman, it is often difficult to tell the difference between an emerging principle of customary international law and what governments may choose to do for particular reasons. Or to put it in more concrete terms, how many interventions in civil conflicts will it take to consolidate an unambiguous right of humanitarian intervention? If it is argued that state practice during the 1990s has already demonstrated that such a right exists, what happens to the law if state practice changes? Still, there is little doubt that there has been a significant shift in public attitudes, at least in Western countries, about sovereign immunity in cases involving gross violations of human rights. Twenty years ago, it would have been virtually unthinkable to have indicted a former head of state in a third country for human rights offences committed while he was in office. It would have been equally unthinkable for NATO to have launched an aerial bombardment of a sovereign country. Yet in the Pinochet case, the British House of Lords voted six to one that the indictment was lawful. Similarly, many international lawyers supported the NATO bombardment of Yugoslavia, over Kosovo.

We do not know if the apparent change from the sanctity of sovereigns to the sanctity of human rights will harden into an uncontested principle of international law. It is difficult not to be sceptical partly because, as Lord Goff reminded the British Law Lords, 'state immunity is a matter of particular importance to heads of state of powerful countries' whose actions may make them targets of 'governments of states which for deeply felt political reasons deplore their action while in office'.[2] It is also difficult to avoid the conclusion that, had an uncontested right of humanitarian intervention already emerged, governments would have weakened in their opposition to secessionist self-determination. So far, in Yugoslavia, as earlier in Iraq and Bosnia, they have deliberately, if perversely, refused to draw this conclusion.

Regardless of the outcome, the new doctrine clearly has powerful advocates. As William Rees-Mogg described it, the doctrine has two leading characteristics. 'It extends the justification for war from self-defence to defence of human rights inside another state. It leaves the judgement to the individual nation or alliance, and does not refer it to the United Nations or any other international body. It thereby removes both consensus and certainty from international law.'[3] From the perspective of international society, politically this is a high price to pay, even if it is being paid in the name of democratic values. Moreover, some democratically elected governments, such as in India, were amongst the fiercest critics of the NATO campaign in Kosovo.

There is a riposte to this line of argument, although it depends on reasserting the primacy of politics over law in international society. Within the classic account of how the society of states operated, it was often noted that the great powers ascribed to themselves special responsibilities for the maintenance of international order through the balance of power. This might require them to breach international law in order to uphold the edifice on which the law, as all the other institutions of international society, ultimately depended. Now that the central balance has been broken, it could plausibly be argued that there is no alternative but for the remaining superpower, in concert with such of its allies prepared to help, to uphold the new democratic standard in international politics by all necessary means. To have gone to the Security Council over Kosovo would have invited a double veto from Russia and China. So, on this view, it was necessary to do what had to be done unilaterally, and to rely on the emerging legal doctrine of humanitarian intervention for justification.

One can have sympathy with this argument, insofar as the concept of international society predates the establishment of the United Nations, and should not be regarded as a synonym for it. If international society cannot be made more responsive to human rather than state needs by consensus, because of a runaway free-rider problem, then the democratic powers must act in the general as well as in their own interests. At the same time, there are two reasons for concern about the direction that international politics has taken in pursuit of democratic values. The first is the role of force in international relations, the second the issue of moral responsibility. Let us consider each in turn.

The sovereign's right to go to war for reasons of state, rather than in self-defence, was not unambiguously outlawed until 1945. The attempt to establish a new security order may have been thwarted by the Cold War and the ever-ready use of the veto, but it represented the first serious attempt to ensure that force would only be employed to uphold rather than undermine international peace and security. That was why the reinvigoration of the Security Council after 1985, and in particular the support that was mobilized in the Council, for Operation Desert Storm, gave rise to such optimism about the prospect for a genuine improvement in international relationships.

In part IV of this book I shall examine the reasons why support for an enhanced security role for the United Nations subsequently eroded. Suffice it to say that it was not because regional organizations such as NATO or the Economic Community of West African States (ECO-WAS) have demonstrated that they have a clearer understanding of how to intervene effectively in civil conflicts where the parties have not committed themselves to a credible cease-fire let alone the search for a political solution. From this point of view, NATO's decision to take action against Yugoslavia in 1999 without Security Council approval almost certainly damaged the reputation of the Council, or at least made it less likely that other states will look to it when faced with either traditional security threats, or engulfed in a humanitarian catastrophe of their own making. It is not yet clear that the situation has been fully retrieved by the action taken in East Timor a few months later.

The attempt to remove war from the arsenal of foreign policy instruments was originally a reflection of the liberal democratic revulsion against the doctrines of power politics that were held responsible for the First World War and fascist expansionism. Indeed, there is a sense in which the political objective of all wars since the American entry into the Second World War has been to create the conditions for democratic reconstruction. The breakdown of internal order in many post-communist third world states after 1989 was seen as threatening not merely the process of democratization in these states themselves, but the stability of neighbouring democratic states also, who were suddenly faced with a flood of refugees. It was this combination of humanitarian concern and fear of the political consequences that led, more by accident than design, to the expanded notion of international peace and security.

The problem is, of course, that under some circumstances the cure of democratization can be worse than the authoritarian disease. As the Secretary-General put it in his 1996 Report to the General Assembly: 'Both democratisation and democracy raise difficult questions of prioritisation and timing. It is therefore not surprising that the acceleration of democratisation and the renaissance of the idea of democracy have met with some resistance.' Behind the bland euphemisms of UN prose, one may detect a perfectly sensible plea for caution in the diplomatic pursuit of democracy whether bilaterally or through international organizations.

So far as the latter are concerned, expansion of UN peace keeping and peace building went hand in hand with diplomatic efforts to promote human rights, the rule of law and democratization. To quote a later report of Secretary-General Annan on this subject: 'Recent developments in many countries demonstrate that an effective system for protecting human rights, including the rule of law, is an indispensable condition for stopping the vicious cycle of violence and conflict, and thus for ensuring

democratic development.'⁴ Whether this somewhat circu-
lar piece of reasoning is true or not, it certainly represents
a sufficiently strong consensus to have persuaded all but
the strongest of undemocratic states such as China, or the
most isolated such as Myanmar, or those which have
effectively collapsed such as Somalia, to go through the
motions of creating a more open society.

The motives of different governments in seeking to
establish their democratic credentials are no doubt mixed.
For some, like Mozambique or possibly Cambodia, it may
be to resolve a deep-seated structural conflict; for others,
like Kenya, it may be the minimum that has to be done to
satisfy international creditors; while in others, Fiji perhaps
or Nigeria or apartheid South Africa in the last days of the
white regime, the political class may be driven by a desire
to overcome its diplomatic isolation. But however unher-
oic the motives, the fact that the United Nations supports
their efforts – since 1989 it has received over 140 requests
for electoral assistance alone and is heavily involved in
providing technical assistance in all aspects of democratization – seals them with a stamp of legitimacy. It is easier
to carry through reforms which are endorsed by an international organization of which one is a member than when
they are extracted by stronger powers in return for some
economic or political concession. If the Western powers
turn their backs on the UN in the security field – and
arguably they have already demonstrated a disproportion-
ate concern for the plight of the Kosovars when compared
with their neglect of the situation in Rwanda, Myanmar
or Sierra Leone – they put at risk their more general
interest in the incremental liberalization of political conditions everywhere.

Without the support of the United Nations, moreover,
bilateral efforts to export democracy by diplomatic means
– generally through aid conditionality or sanctions – are

likely not only to be resented by those on the receiving end, but also to be frustrated. Sometimes this will be because of a lack of information about what can realistically be expected and sometimes because of a lack of capacity even when the government of the targeted state is anxious to comply.

There can be no doubt that, by the end of the Cold War, in many countries the state had become paralyzed by a swollen bureaucracy and the political kleptocracy that controlled it. But, even before political conditionality was added to the economic conditions attached to structural adjustment programmes, the effect of rolling back the state in countries where it lacked deep indigenous roots was sometimes to roll it virtually out of existence. The forces of globalization – including a world-wide trading regime policed by the WTO – will also inevitably create losers as well as winners. In these circumstances there is a real need for the United Nations, as well as for other organizations such as the Commonwealth, to provide a forum where the special difficulties of the weaker states can be examined. If the channels between north and south are not kept open on the basis of mutual respect, the alternative will be the creation of a democratic affluent citadel, surrounded by a brutal and criminalized hinterland, whose unfortunate population will have to be kept out – indeed are already being kept out by force.

The use of economic sanctions to change the behaviour of delinquent states – a kind of democratic surrogate for siege warfare – has always been more popular with governments than academics. The practical problems of sanctions are well known: they seldom achieve their stated objectives, they are difficult to police effectively, and it is virtually impossible to achieve universality in the face of the interest that some states will always have in breaking

ranks in order to profit at others' expense. In the Cold
War, when governments felt compelled to take some
action in response to crises where the use of force risked
. an unacceptable escalation, sanctions could at least be
justified on opportunity cost grounds. But as a weapon in
the battle for a democratic world order they will surely
prove ineffective.

Sanctions might be expected to work best against democratic wrongdoers, since in this case it would be reasonable to assume a link between the electorate and its
representatives. But against tyrannical regimes that have
no compunction in clinging on to power while imposing
the costs on their long-suffering populations, they are
likely to have perverse effects. The experience of both
Iraq and Yugoslavia suggests that, although sanctions
undoubtedly raise the cost of defying the international
community, they provide valuable propaganda advantages
to targeted rulers, who are able to blame the economic
plight of their people on foreign aggressors. As the experience of the Commonwealth has shown, even where the
member-states have committed themselves explicitly
to protect democratic values and have set up a body to
monitor persistent violators and to bring the miscreants
to heel, it requires much more than the imposition of
sanctions. If Nigeria is anything to go by, the foreign
ministers' need the intervention of divine providence – the
death of the President, General Abacha, in 1998 created
the possibility of a return to civilian rule – and a prudent
willingness to overlook all round rigging in the subsequent
elections. With the UN, which does not similarly have to
justify itself in terms of a common political programme,
the task is far more difficult. There is some evidence that
the ethical and practical problems involved in the imposition of sanctions are now being recognized. Again, without
the restraints imposed on states by the United Nations,

there will be increased incentives for their use for short-run political reasons.

This danger may well increase where decentralization accompanies democratization. In many parts of the world this is both a sensible and a necessary approach if government is to be made more accountable to the people. But democracy is notoriously fickle. Because it relies upon public opinion – that is, on the willingness of people to change their minds about who should govern them – it has potential for doing harm as well as good.

This is a general problem of democratic government. It would be naive to assume that it will disappear if government is made more approachable via decentralization, however desirable this might be on other grounds. When, in Ibsen's *An Enemy of the People*, Dr Stockmann accuses the liberals of being the enemies of freedom and insists that the majority never has right on its side, it is local democracy he had in his sights.[5] Already in the United States, which has long been more ready than most countries to impose sanctions unilaterally, state and even city governments have started to impose their own more severe embargoes and boycotts when they consider the measures adopted by the Federal Government to be inadequate or ineffective.[6] It is not a reassuring prospect.

A discussion of the inadequacies of sanctions theory may seem a strange point to arrive at in a discussion of the place of democracy in international society. But it illustrates what seems to me a general weakness in liberal international theory. The original way of settling intractable conflicts of interests was trial by combat. To the liberal mind it is anathema, partly because it personalizes what should be impersonal and partly because it concedes that a right may be derived from an act of violence, in other words, from a wrong. Yet it had at least the advantage that the antagonists took their fate in their own

hands, and accepted responsibility for the consequences
of their actions. Where trial by combat is the final moral
arbiter, there is no room for limited liability. The contrast
is between sudden death and an agreement in advance
that even the loser will not get seriously hurt.

It is perhaps no accident that the same civilization that
developed the concept of limited liability as a way of
persuading individuals to accept risk and responsibility in
the public interest, without putting themselves in jeopardy, should have transformed the ancient art of siege
warfare – the deliberate use of violence to enforce submission through starvation – into economic sanctions.
These are usually represented as a form of peaceful
change. It would be more accurate, however, to describe
them as a form of invisible violence where the responsibility is shifted onto the victims and often barely acknowledged by the instigators. It seems to me that there is a
parallel process at work in the attempt to transform international society from a pluralist association of states into
a solidarist community of democratic peoples.

The danger in both cases arises from a familiar form of
liberal utopianism: the attempt to improve the world not
so much by effort as by rules, procedures, institutions,
and underpinning them all by the correct application of
liberal precepts. Liberals want a mechanical – built-in –
technological solution to human problems. The economic
order that will deliver not merely prosperity but peace and
security (and hence eventually do away with the need to
waste money on armed forces) was identified by David
Ricardo and treated as an article of faith by Richard
Cobden. Something approaching it is now being policed
by the WTO. The political order that will secure people
in their fundamental rights and freedoms was developed
during the French and American revolutions, elevated
into an international doctrine for the reform of inter-

national society by Woodrow Wilson, and revived after the Cold War by the Western democracies and the United Nations.

It is, by and large, a noble vision, and certainly one to be preferred over the bleak prospect of clashing civilizations or a humanity waiting to be unified by a galactic invasion. But it is full of contradictions. It is also constantly weakened by the temptations faced by the most powerful states to go for a quick fix. It is a terrible indictment of the democratic world order that its belief in technological solution to human problems persuaded NATO that it could bomb Yugoslavia into respect for fundamental human rights, while fearful respect for what Western electorates would and would not tolerate, led them into the enterprise without first planning for the ground force that every kind of expert, and a great many ordinary citizens, knew perfectly well would be required from the start.

9

Pluralism and Solidarism Revisited

The previous two chapters have already drawn attention to some of the conceptual and practical obstacles to the democratization of international society. Obstacles, however, can be overcome – they are not prohibitions. With this in mind, we can now return to an earlier question: is the exercise of sovereignty now conditional on a commitment to multi-party democracy? If it is, then it would be safe to conclude that the traditional pluralism of international society, with its modest aim of creating a framework for co-operation between states, will have begun to yield to something approaching a global civil society.

A glance at the way in which the fall of Suharto was handled in Indonesia in 1998, or at how China continues to deal with the United States and other permanent members of the Security Council without having to make serious concessions over human rights, might suggest a sceptical answer. However, even if democracy cannot rank with sovereignty as one of Europe's most successful exports to the rest of the world, its appeal should not be discounted altogether. In an era of rapid global communications, ideas can spread with the speed of an infectious virus, even if they are also liable to mutate in the process.

It was probably inevitable that Western Europe and North America would set the agenda for the post-Cold

War world. The ancient way of settling disputes about fundamentals – trial by combat – has survived into the modern world, albeit in an unacknowledged and somewhat emasculated form.[1] The Western democracies won the Second World War and by this victory earned the right to determine the shape of the new order. The West European countries are also the only regional group of states to have succeeded from the beginning – first in the Council of Europe, then in the European Community/Union – in basing their own co-operation on a shared adherence to democratic principles. With the collapse of communism there was no other large-scale ideological vision left in the political marketplace. Nonetheless, democratic triumphalism after the Cold War was unfortunate: it suggested that all that was necessary to secure a democratic world order was a commitment to solidarist principles, multi-party elections and an act of political will. There was a tendency to gloss over the very high price the Europeans had paid (and inflicted upon the rest of the world) in establishing their own version of the democratic peace.

It is also far from certain that the Western powers have abandoned the pluralist conception of international society which was the most lasting legacy of the Westphalian settlement. When Henry Adams was sent as ambassador to France, he failed to secure French agreement to create a revolutionary concert supported by a completely open trans-national market. The French were more interested in negotiating, on the traditional basis of inter-governmental reciprocity, monopoly trading rights in and out of Boston harbour.[2] Two hundred years later, Margaret Thatcher and François Mitterrand reacted angrily when the United States attempted to extend its jurisdiction extra-territorially in an unsuccessful attempt to prevent British and French participation in the construction of the Friendship gas pipeline from the Soviet Union to Western Europe.[3] In other words, even amongst democratic allies, non-interference continued to be regarded as the essential aspect of sovereignty, in the context of international co-operation. Without it, governments would have no defence against more powerful states, acting outside agreed alliance objectives, when national interests were perceived to conflict.

These observations suggest that when UN Secretary-General Boutros-Ghali called for democracy within 'communities, within states and within the community of states', in his *Agenda for Peace*, he was talking of different, if overlapping, phenomena. 'Democracy within communities' presumably referred to entrenching fundamental human rights and providing for participation in local affairs on a non-discriminatory basis. 'Democracy within states' clearly referred to the constitutional arrangements under which the people freely choose their own governments, and have a regular opportunity to replace them. 'Democracy within the community of states', on the other hand, is a more ambiguous phrase. Traditionally, it has meant respecting the sovereign equality of states, regardless of the relative power, except where by agreement certain states were given special rights and responsibilities, as in the Security Council with its permanent veto-wielding members. But, in the context of the discussion of self-determination in the *Agenda for Peace*, the implication is that democracy is to be treated as one of the fundamental, and hence defining, values of international society.

If the conventional post-1945 interpretation of self-determination as decolonization is adopted, there is little, if anything, beyond exhortation, that can be done at the international level to bring about local or national democracy where it does not already exist. The equal rights of all members of the United Nations protect them from external interference in their domestic arrangements. If, on the other hand, self-determination is to be reinterpreted as democratic government within existing borders, as a fundamental value of international society, we have to ask what the international community should do to promote democratization.

There are two possible courses of action, corresponding very broadly to the measures envisaged in chapters 6 and 7 of the UN Charter in the context of peaceful conflict resolution and enforcement. First, where requested, international organizations can and do provide technical assistance in facilitating the transition from military or authoritarian government to an open system. Such assistance is provided not only by the United Nations itself, but by regional organizations and by the Commonwealth. Secondly, where the transition turns out to be a source of conflict rather than its solution as a result of ethnic or communal conflict, the international community may be drawn in militarily to protect the victims.

The second – and more problematic – of these interventions is the subject of part IV of this book. For the moment let us concentrate on the first. Retraining the judiciary in the habits of independence, introducing legislators to best practice in parliamentary procedure, drawing up electoral rolls, monitoring elections and providing their outcome with a seal of approval, all this can be criticized for mistaking appearance for substance, or for allowing unscrupulous or opportunist leaders to repackage their regimes in order to cling onto power and win international approval; but it is difficult to believe that it does much harm and it may do some good. Shame and honour should not be lightly dismissed as the supports of a new democratic standard. Leaders may choose to flout values espoused by their peers, but they would usually prefer not to. Democratic culture may also have to develop indigenous roots, but in the meantime the need to meet certain minimal standards of good governance may purchase them some time in which to do so. And if it saves some relatively innocent people from persecution, torture or worse, in a non-ideal world, the exercise will surely have been worthwhile.

The technical capacity of the United Nations to deal with complex emergencies has been greatly improved as a result of the experience of the 1990s. In 1997 a report by a high-level group, commissioned by United Nations Association of the USA, made further recommendations on this score.[4] But – as its authors readily admit – capacity building, at the UN, within regional organizations or elsewhere, can do little to address the underlying problem of political will, or more accurately its absence. The international community has shown little inclination to establish a new system of trusteeships for collapsed states. Without state authority, how can the democratic right of self-determination within existing borders be protected, let alone the people secured against systematic human rights abuse? The Commonwealth's efforts to transform itself into an association of democratic states, and to persuade military regimes to conduct elections and implement the Harare Declaration, have arguably met with some success. However, in the cases of Nigeria and Sierra Leone, both of which returned to civilian rule at the end of the 1990s, it is difficult to assess what role international pressure played in securing this outcome. No doubt it played some role, if only to encourage local activists. In Pakistan, since 1998 a nuclear power, international pressure failed to deter the military, which overthrew the elected, although discredited, government in a popular *coup d'état* in September 1999. Whether suspension from 'the Councils of the Commonwealth' – a form of words that was deliberately chosen to keep the door open for Commonwealth mediation – will have any effect remains to be seen. International pressure may have been one factor in persuading the military government from suspending the constitution, although it seems more likely that this concession was directed at the authorities in Washington rather than the Commonwealth secretariat in London.

An international society reconstructed on the solidarist principles of respect for human rights and democratic government would come close to being a world empire achieved by consent or, in Kantian terms, a self-policing Perpetual Peace. A world of this kind would not need the apparatus of imperial rule. If a democratic world order cannot be brought about by military intervention, and if it cannot be upheld – even in extreme cases of anarchy – by imperial means, however benign their intent, what sanctions can or should be applied to bring delinquent states to their solidarist senses? As we saw in the previous chapter this is a normative question posed by the prospect of internationally sponsored democratization.

Even when sanctions seem successful in helping to return a country to democracy, as in Haiti in 1994, they remain morally dubious. In that case, they undoubtedly increased the level of suffering of the population, but were considered necessary as a prelude to the Security Council resolutions authorizing military intervention, which in turn helped to restore the legitimate and elected government to power.[5] It is difficult to square such actions with the Kantian injunction to treat people as ends in themselves and not merely as a means to some end, however desirable. As an international policy, the promotion of democratization through coercive action, is thus mired in contradiction.

In the contest between the solidarist and pluralist conceptions of international society, it seems that the pluralists still hold the ascendancy. This is a long way from saying that solidarist arguments have been driven from the field. It merely indicates that any expansion of international co-operation, beyond the law of coexistence and inter-state reciprocity, can only be achieved by consensus, and therefore, almost certainly, also incrementally. In these circumstances the attempt to reinterpret the right of all peoples to self-determination as democratic self-government has focused attention on minorities for the first time since 1945.

The reason is straightforward. To recapitulate the argument from the earlier discussion of self-determination: if many societies are, as a matter of observable and experienced fact, deeply divided, the transition to democracy will abort for the reasons so accurately foreseen by Mill. Yet the creation of new states by secession or partition can rarely be achieved without unleashing ferocious conflict, and not often even then. Why this should be is, ultimately, mysterious, but it seems to have something to do with the sacralization of territory under conditions of popular sovereignty. The case for accepting the new, non-statist, definition of self-determination as democratic self-government is that there is no escape from the arbitrary and contingent nature of political boundaries. It follows that what is required is constitutional engineering to reassure minorities that they will not be discriminated against and that their interests and identities will be protected.

The first attempt to build a principle of minority protection into the constitution of international society foundered between the two world wars. This was partly because it was not universally applied – and those countries whose membership of the League of Nations was dependent on their signing treaties guaranteeing minority rights understandably resented being treated differently from other states. It was also because, as Jennifer Jackson-Preece has noted, the principle was discredited after it was used by the Third Reich 'to justify the dismemberment of Czechoslovakia in 1938, the transfer of southern Slovakia and half of Transylvania to Hungary in 1940, and the creation of Slovak and Croat puppet states'.[6] After 1945 international concern for minorities was largely replaced by, and subsumed within, the Universal Declaration of Human Rights and its supporting covenants.

The second attempt, after the Cold War, was a significant if limited improvement. The 1992 UN Declaration on the Rights of Persons Belonging to National or Ethnic, Religious and Linguistic Minorities was proclaimed by the General Assembly and was, therefore, in principle applicable to all states. By adding to the rights stipulated in Article 27 of the International Covenant on Civil and Political Rights[7] the right of minorities 'to participate in relevant national and regional decisions, to establish and maintain associations, and to have contact both within and across international frontiers', it also constituted 'a floor for international thinking on minority questions . . . Other regional organisations – whether in Europe or indeed elsewhere – might agree on something better than this basic code . . . but they could not go beneath it'. The improvement on earlier efforts to make minority protection an international norm is limited by the lack of enforcement measures. And this weakness in turn reflects the determination of governments to give no encouragement to minority secession or irredentism. A close reading of this and similar texts suggests that any development of international society along solidarist lines will only be entertained if it is explicitly balanced by prior commitment to maintain the pluralist compact.

In Europe, where the problem of reconciling national

self-determination with minority protection first originated, considerable progress was achieved at the political
level within the European Union, the Council of Europe
and the Organization for Security and Co-operation in
Europe (OSCE). An impressive series of Declarations,
Documents and Conventions was negotiated between
1990 and 1995. The OSCE also created the office of High
Commissioner for National Minorities to monitor member states' performance and to engage in preventative
diplomacy. Significantly, however, although the High
Commissioner is empowered to investigate any situation
which he considers has a potential for conflict, and to
make recommendations to governments based on his
findings, once a conflict becomes violent, he is grounded.
The reason, presumably, is that mediation in a violent
civil conflict could be construed as equal recognition of
the rights of the rebellious minority and the government.

The 1993 Council of Europe's decision to draw up a
Convention on National Minorities (which is open to all
European states whether members of the Council or not)
has been implemented. In contrast little progress has been
made with their simultaneous decision to draw up a
National Minorities Protocol to the European Convention
on Human Rights. Two reasons are probably responsible
for the reluctance of governments to pursue this initiative.
The first is an intellectual difference over the nature of the
minority problem and hence the appropriate legal instrument to overcome it. For those who believe that minority
problems arise from discrimination by the majority, protection of individual rights, usually by entrenching them
in the constitution, and the use of the law to prevent
discrimination, is the necessary but also sufficient
response. On the other hand, there are minorities who do
not merely wish to be protected against discrimination but
see the essence of the problem in their need to have their

own cultural distinctiveness protected, and indeed bolstered by the state. They want not merely individual but group rights and entitlements. Secondly, attaching a protocol to the European Convention of Human Rights would de-politicize an issue over which governments are currently determined to retain control, regardless of which side they take in the philosophical dispute. Unless there was to be a public international agreement to reinterpret the right of all peoples to self-determination as a right to democratic self-government – an outcome which seems improbable at the present time – governments will continue to see the spectre of secession and irredentism in any attempt to make minority claims justifiable.

Paradoxically, it is because the organizations representing indigenous peoples have been careful to avoid offending official sensitivities on this score that they have had more success in establishing self-determination as one of their human rights. The definition of an indigenous people is ultimately no more straightforward than the definition of a minority, and for much the same reasons. Neither have been authoritatively defined, but representatives of indigenous peoples insist that they are not minorities and are, in any case, nowhere in a position, numerically or politically, to demand external sovereignty.

On the other hand they have succeeded in having their special status recognized by the international community. The international Labour Organizations' Convention 169 referred to 'their rights to "ownership and possession" of the "total environment" that they occupy or use, as well as their rights to be protected from environmental degradation, involuntary removal and unwanted intrusion by outsiders.'[8] In 1992, the Rio Declaration on Environment and Development recognized 'indigenous peoples as distinct social partners in achieving sustainable development' and called on states 'to recognise and duly support their

identity, culture and interests and to enable their effective
participation' towards this end.

These developments fell short of public acknowledge-
ment of their right to self-determination as distinct 'peoples' – the Charter formula – rather than people requiring
special treatment. This issue proved controversial at the
UN World Conference on Human Rights held in Vienna
in June 1993, for reasons that echo the problems of
defining and entrenching minority rights. Nor have these
problems been finally resolved. However, Article 3 of the
1993 Draft Declaration on the Rights of Indigenous Peoples is unequivocal:

> Indigenous peoples have the right of self-determination. By
> virtue of that right they freely determine their political
> status and freely pursue their economic, social and cultural
> development.[9]

If and when the Declaration is eventually adopted by the
General Assembly, it will still not be binding on states,
although it will arguably become part of the corpus of
'soft international law' and will contribute to the process
of international standard setting. Moreover, even if it is
not adopted in its present form, it seems clear that indigenous peoples have asserted their rights of independent
access to international forums, and to that extent have
successfully challenged the state's monopoly on sovereignty. It is ironic, but apparently the case, that, outside
the European Union, which uniquely straddles constitutional and diplomatic norms and arrangements, it is the
world's most vulnerable peoples who have succeeded in
keeping alive the solidarist conception of a wider international society in an otherwise pluralist age. By avoiding
the quagmire of definition, the representatives of indigenous peoples made significant political gains. But three

aspects of their campaign suggest that the battle is far from over.

First, it is no accident that the campaign was initiated by indigenous groups in North America and other countries of European settlement. Many of these groups ceded sovereignty to their conquerors under treaties which, theoretically, guaranteed them in the ownership of their lands and the rights to maintain their traditional customs and institutions. Such treaties were notoriously more often honoured in the breach than in the observance, but their existence meant that once a Western-educated elite emerged, educated in the political theory of both property rights and self-determination, they were also well-placed to press their claims in the appropriate political idiom and on the basis of pre-existing title.

In practice, these claims were usually for compensation in respect of the requisition of land, but it was a short step to the demand for political recognition. Barsh records that at the first meeting of the UN Working Group in 1982 the representative of the Micmaq Nation was quick to expose a fundamental weakness in the conventional interpretation of self-determination as decolonization: 'We must be careful not to apply the principle of self-determination to the wrong people in a colonial situation. It is not de-colonisation but a cruel deception, when self-determination in a colonised country is considered the exclusive prerogative of the colonists' (quoted in Barsh, 'Indigenous Peoples', p. 36).

Secondly, there continues to be strong resistance from India and other Asian countries to the proposition that tribal peoples in their countries – the most numerous group of indigenous peoples world-wide – are covered by the term. The problem here is that while political cultures constantly borrow from one another, they do so selectively. In Europe there is a long-standing, if contested, tradition of resolving the tensions that inevitably arise between civil society (with its roots in the institution of private property) and the state by dividing sovereignty. It was perhaps this tradition that lay behind the British imperial practice of indirect rule and their willingness – as in Buganda or Barotseland – to countenance the idea of a protected state within a colony. In practice a state within a state is what the majority of indigenous self-determination claims amount to. There may, indeed, be intractable problems in meeting these demands, but if they are overcome, there are no insuperable theoretical or constitutional obstacles to constitutional experimentation of this kind within Western political traditions.

There is no reason to believe that the West has a monopoly of constitutional wisdom. All the same, it was sovereignty, in the monarchical and Hobbesian sense of final and exclusive authority, rather than democratic power-sharing or division, which proved the most successful Western export to the rest of the world during the age of imperialism. Consequently, it is in Asia that solidarist arguments for eroding state sovereignty and territorial integrity are viewed with most suspicion. The same would, no doubt, be true of Africa, if the near-collapse of so many states had not dramatically reduced their voice in international affairs. Certainly, even before the 1994 genocide, it would have been hard to conceive of the Tutsi in Rwanda or Burundi conceding any special rights to the Hutu majority on the grounds that they were notionally the aboriginal population.

This fanciful hypothesis throws light on a final confusing aspect of the campaign to re-cast self-determination as internal self-government. Despite the political importance of treating minority rights and the rights of indigenous peoples as separate, it is clear that in practice indigenous peoples are thought of as minorities. But they are also identified by their distinct and premodern way of life, which has survived despite its inevitable penetration and erosion by a myriad of modern influences from contract labour to gambling casinos. The Hutu are disqualified by their majority status and because, despite the persistence of racial stereotypes, their way of life is indistinguishable from the minority Tutsi, many of whom were their neighbours, at the time of the genocide.

It will take more than constitutional engineering to solve the crisis between these two communities. It will need a gigantic transformation in their consciousness and self-identity. Indeed, there is a case for saying that it was premature, in the sense of ill-prepared, plans for power-sharing that triggered the genocide in 1994. But even where an indigenous population retains a distinct identity and culture from later immigrants with whom it shares the country and whose numbers are roughly equivalent, it is not clear that the principle of primordial title will be easy to square with the new conventional interpretation of self-determination as democratic self-government.

When indigenous Fijians staged a coup against the elected (Indian-dominated) government in 1987, their membership of the United Nations was not affected. Because at that time the government of India was prominent in the anti-apartheid campaign within the Commonwealth, they were forced out of that organization. A decade later – after much regional and Commonwealth diplomacy – they returned following the negotiation of a new constitution which aimed to reconcile their rights with those of the population as a whole. They were suspended a second time – but for the same reason – in the summer of 2000. These episodes can be read two ways. They may be interpreted as symptomatic of a general trend towards defining the nation in civic terms and protecting ethnic and communal identities by constitutional means, thus in effect diluting the external sovereignty of the state. Alternatively, the international response may be interpreted as the result of a unique conjunction of events and pressures from which it is impossible to draw any generally applicable lessons.

The first Fijian crisis occurred before the end of the Cold War – although at a time when its melancholy disciplines were already being relaxed – and was, in any case, not accompanied by the massive displacement and inter-communal slaughter that were the defining characteristics of the crises of the 1990s. It was these that raised the final question for our reappraisal of international society at the Millennium. What should the international community do to protect the victims of such disasters when the perpetrators are their own governments, or even sometimes the people themselves?

Part IV

Intervention

10

Intervention in Liberal International Theory

The last decade of the twentieth century opened and closed with wars that were ended as the result of international interventions. Operation Desert Storm, which ousted Iraq from Kuwait in January 1991, was an American-led, predominantly Western, military campaign. But it was mounted with a mandate under Chapter VII of the UN Charter, with the unanimous support of the Security Council, and the enthusiastic backing of all the Middle Eastern states, ironically with the exception of the West's closest regional ally, Jordan. NATO's bombardment of former Yugoslavia in March 1999 succeeded in forcing the Serbs out of Kosovo after a bombing campaign of seventy-nine days. It was again led by the United States but this time without recourse to the Security Council and in the face of considerable international criticism.

The Gulf War was initially fought to reverse an aggression, not for humanitarian reasons. Indeed, many of those opposed to the war pointed out, at the time, that Kuwait's human rights record left much to be desired. But Saddam Hussein's brutal suppression of the northern Kurdish and southern Shi'ite rebellions, after the war, led the Western powers to risk offending some of their erstwhile supporters by their decision to establish safe havens for both communities. These actions took place in a country whose aggressive designs against a neighbour has been legally repulsed, but not in one whose sovereignty or territorial integrity had been formally revoked. These interventions were not only justified on humanitarian grounds: their 'success' gave rise to the hope that, in the post-Cold War climate, it would be possible for the international community, acting through the Security Council, to intervene in civil conflicts to protect the victims of sustained human rights abuse, even when the perpetrators were their own governments.

Despite this enthusiasm, which was initially shared by the three Western permanent members of the Council, from the start there were dissenting voices. For this reason, the Western powers relied, somewhat dubiously, on previous Security Council resolutions to justify their actions within Iraq – they knew that several non-permanent members, including India and Zimbabwe, would have opposed any resolution that legitimized interference in the domestic affairs of a sovereign state and that China might well have vetoed it.

By contrast, NATO justified its intervention in Yugoslavia as a humanitarian operation from the start. In the words of the British Defence Secretary, George Robertson, it was fought 'to avert a humanitarian catastrophe by disrupting the violent attacks currently being carried out by the Yugoslav security forces against the Kosovo Albanians and to limit their ability to conduct such repression in the future'.[1] On closer inspection, the two episodes reveal more continuity than change in the theory and practice of humanitarian intervention. It is true that, in Kosovo, the United Nations was only involved at the close of the campaign, while in northern Iraq the Western powers argued that their actions were covered by a previous Security Council resolution (688), passed in the context of the war over Kuwait. But, more significantly, in neither case were they prepared to seek a new Security Council Resolution under Chapter VII, for fear – and in the latter case the certainty – of facing a veto.

In the period between the Gulf War and the Kosovo crisis, the United Nations was involved in an unprecedented number of conflicts – fourteen in Africa alone.[2] The majority were intra- rather than inter-state conflicts and UN intervention was driven by the need to provide humanitarian relief, alongside, and indeed as an essential ingredient of, more traditional peace-keeping and peace-making functions. However, most of these operations were based on Chapter VI mandates. In other words, they depended on the consent of previously conflicting parties, and, as we shall see, should not strictly speaking be classified as humanitarian interventions. In the minority of operations which were based on a Chapter VII mandate – those in Somalia, Bosnia, Rwanda, Haiti and Albania where the intervening states were authorized to use force to achieve their humanitarian objectives – opinions differ widely on whether the experiment should be counted a success.[3] In Bosnia, the most protracted of these conflicts, the war was only ended after the United States had taken over the diplomatic initiative from the UN and the peace-keeping operation had been taken over by NATO. Moreover, the peace conference held in Dayton, Ohio, in November 1995 was facilitated by the United States and its allies turning a blind eye to Croatia's ethnic cleansing of the Krajina, an action that was hardly consistent with the humanitarian objectives for which the UN operation had originally been established.

Following the signing of the Dayton Accords, the major powers seemed disinclined to continue the debate about the rights and wrongs, and practicality of humanitarian intervention, which had been such a feature of the early 1990s. Western publics – it was said – were suffering from compassion fatigue. The debate was inevitably rekindled, however, by the NATO action against Yugoslavia over its treatment of the Kosovo Albanians. After all, it remained uncomfortably true that most of the refugees, whose return was NATO's major stated war aim, had been forced out of Kosovo after the beginning of the bombing campaign. The humanitarian motives of the NATO powers are not in doubt (although they clearly had other powerful motives as well). What remains in doubt is whether humanitarian intervention is consistent with the prevailing norms of international society. In order to answer this question, it will be helpful to locate it within the theory of international relations from which it derives.

The concept of humanitarian intervention occupies an ambiguous place in the theory and practice of international society. At first sight this may seem counterintuitive since in other areas of social life, for example medicine or public health, advances in welfare and the accompanying reduction of unnecessary suffering could not have been achieved without human intervention. Extreme advocates of *laissez-faire* may cling to the view that social and economic progress has depended on governments refraining from interference in the market, but even a cursory examination of the record will prove them wrong. There is a genuine argument about the balance of private and public interventions which is most likely to maximize welfare in particular circumstances, but few economists would seriously maintain that economic growth is a purely natural phenomenon. Only in international relations does the concept of intervention retain its sinister reputation.

The reason is not mysterious. It flows from the fact that the modern international system has been constructed on the basis of the principle of sovereignty, and its twin entailments, territorial integrity and non-interference in the domestic affairs of other states. Sovereignty is the corner-stone not only of international law but of the diplomatic system. It is sometimes argued that economic globalization has made this system obsolete – that the money that lubricates the contemporary world is no more respectful of international borders than the tsetse fly. This argument should not be taken too seriously. Trans-national market integration, which was predicted by every major political economist from Adam Smith to Karl Marx, may indeed have made it more difficult for national governments to exercise sovereign authority, but it has done nothing to replace them with an alternative structure. In any case, the rules that have been established in an attempt to level the playing field for international trade and monetary transactions – for example under the WTO – have been negotiated and entered into voluntarily by sovereign states. It is simply misleading to regard all action beyond the borders of the state as intervention. It is only when a doctor embarks upon a treatment expressly against the will of the patient that intervention becomes problematic. In international society the states are the wilful patients but there are no doctors. Similarly, intervention becomes problematic when it goes against the sovereign will of the state. Indeed, it is for this reason that the term is normally confined to coercive action to make another government – or armed movement – do something it would not otherwise choose to do.

The states-system developed in its modern form as a self-help system. The Peace of Westphalia established a quasi-constitutional order, which outlawed religious war but was in other respects highly permissive. The formula *cuius regio eius religio*, the ancestor clause to the modern non-interference principle, left sovereigns free to pursue their interests by whatever means they saw fit, up to and including war for reasons of state and territorial conquest.

Grotius and his followers kept alive the medieval tradition of the just war, including the idea that states should be entitled to intervene in order to prevent oppression and maltreatment in other states. But as the natural law tradition was gradually taken over by the modern conception of positive international law, they became more concerned with developing the concept of a fair fight – *ius in bello* – in war between European sovereigns than with *ius ad bellum* – the requirement that the war itself should be just. Further afield, for example in the competition between the Dutch and Portuguese to establish a monopoly over the spice trade in the East Indies or in the creation of plantation economies in the new world on the basis of imported African slave labour, the European powers showed little restraint under either head. Non-intervention, it seemed, was consistent with a system of power politics. Humanitarian considerations were seldom referred to, and before the end of the nineteenth century were never entertained as a justification for the introduction of outside force into civil conflicts.

All political action involves a contest, not merely to effect outcomes, in other words to shape the human environment according to certain ideas about justice and order, but to do so in an authoritative manner. Politics cannot be divorced from power, but without authority, power is bound to degenerate into a conflict in which there is neither justice nor order. This familiar liberal maxim has never stopped ambitious and ruthless men from seeking power for its own sake, but it continues nonetheless to underpin all liberal thought about government and international relations. Its implications in the two spheres, however, are different.

In the domestic sphere, sovereignty can be exercised either by prescriptive right, or under representative arrangements designed to reflect 'the will of the people'.

Since the French and American revolutions prescription –
most often expressed by dynastic rule – has increasingly
given way to various forms of popular sovereignty. We
have already noted the conceptual incoherence inherent
in the right of national self-determination, namely the
impossibility of arriving at an objective criterion that
would allow us to distinguish between those groups which
can legitimately claim this right, and those which cannot.
The most recent attempt to overcome this difficulty has
been to redefine it as a right to democratic self-government within existing international borders. This might
conceivably work if everyone agreed to it. But even where
they do, the difficulties inherent in finding a democratic
formula which will fit all national and cultural circumstances has allowed unofficial political dynasties and/or
self-perpetuating political oligarchies to re-establish themselves in many countries.

Empirical problems of this kind do not in themselves
undermine the traditional liberal understanding of international society. Whether rule is exercised by prescription
or on the basis of real or merely putative representation,
from one point of view makes little difference: either way
sovereign powers are ultimately accountable to the people
over whom they exercise their authority. In democratic
countries they can be removed through the ballot box; in
authoritarian states, if the government systematically
oppresses the bulk of the population – unhappily, minorities are another matter – it will eventually face a popular
insurrection. Internally, it is thus ultimately the ethic of
responsibility that justifies the self-help system.

Liberal thought has more difficulty in dealing with a
concept of self-help at the international level. This is
because, until the end of the nineteenth century, once
across the border, self-help was more often than not
translated as help-yourself. Colonial expansion had not

seriously troubled the European conscience, because in a
mercantilist age it was taken for granted that there would
always be winners and losers. A zero-sum world view
might not be very edifying but that was the way the world
was assumed to be. Under dynasticism, people had at best
very limited political and civil rights – and in many
countries none at all; consequently European governments did not have to fear charges of double standards.

All this changed in the course of the nineteenth century.
Western imperialism was now paradoxically driven forward by the two leading European democracies, Britain
and France. For a time, they were able to justify their
enclosure of the non-European world by theories which
sought to explain Western dominance by analogy to Dar-
win's theory of natural selection. But, however convenient, social Darwinism was never convincing. Once
ideas of equality before the law, and equal civil and
political rights, had been entrenched in the metropolitan
countries themselves, it was only a matter of time before
the discriminatory treatment of colonial subjects would
appear contradictory, not merely to the victims, whose
knowledge of their situation was brought home to them
by exposure to Western education and values, but to the
imperialists themselves.

In *A Few Words on Non-Intervention*, John Stuart Mill
defended the British annexation of the independent
princely state of Oudh (present-day Uttar Pradesh). Mill
argued that, just because Britain exercised absolute
authority in the surrounding territory, and had, therefore,
effectively released the ruler from the necessity of providing for the defence of his own country, it could not
simultaneously rely on the doctrine of non-interference in
an attempt to escape responsibility for the destitution into
which the ruler had allowed his country to fall. There was,
Mill implied, a moral obligation on Britain to intervene

for humanitarian reasons. I shall return to the relevance of this argument to contemporary debates on humanitarian intervention. Here the point to note is that, while in domestic politics it is accepted that governments must be held accountable for their actions, in line with the ethic of self-help, Mill's argument has not been widely used by those wishing to claim a right of humanitarian intervention. Most twentieth-century liberal thinkers have been reluctant to follow his logic, presumably because of the difficulty of distinguishing between humanitarian and less worthy motives for intervention. Indeed, at the international level, non-intervention, like non-discrimination in economic affairs, is generally assumed to be an impeccably liberal principle.

With a Millian approach to the problem of humanitarian intervention blocked off, the question has been discussed, on the one hand, in terms of the duties of governments to uphold the inalienable human rights of those under their charge, and, on the other, of the recognition that there may be some violations of these rights which are so massive as to justify a breach of the non-intervention principle under exceptional circumstances. Theoretically, these two positions are not mutually exclusive, but in practice those who stress the first tend to see international law as the primary instrument for developing international society along progressive lines, while those who accept that it is impossible – and indeed undesirable – for the law to cover all contingencies, regard the law as a pivotal institution of international society, but in the final analysis only one of several such institutions. In short, the first group work within a legalist paradigm, the second within a political one.

The failure of legalism between the two world wars led to a reassertion of the primacy of politics, and, through the institution of the Security Council, the recognition of

the special responsibility of the great powers for international order. Paradoxically, it was these same powers
that were responsible for promulgating two new international crimes – crimes against humanity and war crimes.
It was also the great powers which, in 1948, secured the
passage of the Genocide Convention, which sought to
establish the prevention and punishment of genocide as a
peremptory norm of international law.

It could be argued that the post-1945 international
society was deliberately reconstructed to uphold the principle of state sovereignty, but also on occasion to allow it
to be breached. However, whether as a consequence of
the Cold War or for other reasons, between 1949 and
1990 such breaches of the non-intervention rule as
occurred – and there were many – were not justified on
humanitarian grounds. In those cases where such a
defence could most plausibly have been offered – in the
Indian intervention on behalf of the Bengali separatists of
East Pakistan, in Tanzania's deposition of the Ugandan
dictator, Idi Amin, and in Vietnam's action against Pol
Pot's genocidal regime in Cambodia – it was not. Indeed,
in the last case, the Western powers refused to accept the
legitimacy of the regime imposed by the Vietnamese to
replace Pol Pot so long as the Cold War lasted. By 1989
the majority of governments had ratified the Universal
Declaration of Human Rights and its two supporting
covenants, but this did not prevent them from sheltering,
with impunity, behind Articles 2.4 and 2.7 of the Charter.

Thus after 1945 international society was reconstructed
on the basis of an unequal compromise between power
and law. Under it, the use of force, other than in self-
defence, was to be sanctioned only on the authority of the
Security Council and only then when the Council determined that a threat to international peace and security
existed and that all alternative means of settlement had

been exhausted. There was also provision for a reference to the Security Council under the Genocide Convention, presumably in the expectation – although this interpretation has never been tested – that it would rule that genocide, although carried out within the borders of a state, could nonetheless justify action under Chapter VII of the Charter. In other words, it was tacitly accepted that deciding when to trigger the collective security provisions of the Charter could not be determined by objective criteria, and without reference to the national interests of the major powers.

11

Humanitarian Intervention in the 1990s

If this account of the underlying rationale of liberal thought on intervention is broadly accepted, it remains to ask whether it has been modified by events since the end of the Cold War. The collapse of communism and the disintegration of the Soviet Union was a world historical event, not merely in the trite sense that nobody predicted it, but because its effects were felt throughout the international system. It was followed by a series of violent conflicts in many parts of the world, which, in turn, provided the setting for an unprecedented series of UN interventions. Most of these fell somewhere between traditional peace keeping and peace enforcement under Chapter VII of the Charter. There are those who argue that none of these operations was either appropriate or successful.[1] Nonetheless, where they followed, rather than accompanied, the negotiation of a political settlement – as in Namibia, Cambodia and Mozambique – UN forces were able to reinforce the work of humanitarian agencies and contribute to political stabilization. On the other hand, where the humanitarian catastrophe was the direct result of the absence of any such settlement – or at least one to which the parties were seriously committed – UN intervention probably had more negative than positive results.

The reluctance of the major powers to sanction new peace-keeping operations in the second half of the 1990s reflects this view. Throughout this period the United Nations was in financial crisis, not least because of the arrears owed by the United States, which refused to pay for programmes that did not enjoy Congressional support but was also reluctant to consider any change in UN financing that might reduce its own influence. The decline of Security Council activism may be partly attributable to this situation. But, since the entire UN peace-keeping budget at the end of the 1990s amounted to less than the cost of two days of fighting in the Gulf War at the beginning, Western reluctance to sanction new UN operations – a reluctance that did not extend to NATO – was clearly only partly explained by budgetary constraints. More centrally, it is related to the discovery, in the Somali and Bosnian conflicts, that there is no Chapter six-and-a half solution. Traditional peace keeping required the consent of the parties and, particularly where the UN was engaged in active peace building as well, their confidence in its impartiality. Enforcement, on the other hand, required partiality, at least at the point of intervention and until those responsible for the crisis have been restrained and persuaded to co-operate.

This observation only seems obvious with hindsight. It was perhaps unfortunate that the UN's new role in the security field should have been tested in two of the most intractable civil conflicts anywhere in the world. In former Yugoslavia, once the overarching federal structure had been removed, the populations of the successor republics refused to accept the legitimacy of their previously internal – but now international – borders. What were formerly inter-state wars (requiring, according to some prominent international lawyers, a similarly robust response as had greeted Saddam Hussein's annexation of Kuwait) had all

the characteristics of a ferocious civil war, in which compromise fails in the face of the passionate and self-right-
eous belief of the belligerents in the justice of their
respective causes.

The result was that even when the Security Council
invoked Chapter VII, it was unable to fashion a mandate
that would allow the UN to do more than soften the worst
consequences of the competitive ethnic cleansing in which
all sides engaged. The preferred American strategy, of air
strikes against the Serbs, whom they identified as the main
culprits, had the advantage of not confusing humanitarian
relief with peace enforcement, but it left those countries
with troops on the ground dangerously exposed to hos-
tage-taking by the Serb-dominated Yugoslav army. The
open disagreement amongst the Western powers about
how to deal with the crisis inevitably whittled away at the
UN's authority.

If the confusion in former Yugoslavia arose from the
fact that the overlapping wars were at once civil and
international, in Somalia the collapse of the state had
much the same effect. In both countries social life was
reduced to the level of a primitive and anarchic state of
war. The international response to the Somali crisis, first
under UNITAF, the American-led task force, and its
successor UNOSOM II, was again framed within Chapter
VII mandates, despite the absence of any major international dimension to the conflict. But in this case the
prospects for the restoration of stability were even bleaker.
In Bosnia, the rival Serb and Croat communities seemed
determined to make their political and communal boundaries congruent, leaving the hapless Bosnian Muslims
trapped in the middle. But, by the same token, this made
the inter-clan conflict in southern Somalia even less sus-
ceptible to an eventual negotiated settlement. Somalia's
inter-clan conflict was less open to external mediation

because, in a still predominantly nomadic country, the competition for power was not primarily territorial. Territory is vital to nomadic peoples, but not in the sense implied by the doctrine of sovereignty, of a ring-fenced enclosure. As a local saying has it, 'wherever the camel roams, that is Somalia'!

However objectionable to liberal sensibilities, territorial partition could at least provide a basis for an eventual settlement in Bosnia. When the UN finally withdrew from Somalia, it left the political situation much as it had found it. It is true that in Bosnia the partition, which reflected the balance of forces after ethnic cleansing, was contained within a loose confederal constitution to retain the illusion of Bosnia's legal personality, and the fiction that international society no longer tolerates the use of force to redraw the political map. However, these devices at least allowed the guns to be silenced.

It is important not to exaggerate the extent of the UN's failure in the interventions of the early 1990s. In both Bosnia and Somalia, lives were saved and the level of suffering reduced as a result of the UN presence. In Somalia, where in order to deliver humanitarian assistance, NGOs had to buy protection with money that was then used to purchase the weapons and supplies that fed the conflict, the worst aspects of this vicious circle were broken. The failure was political, not humanitarian: those targeted were not coerced into changing their objectives, with the result that the major powers came to fear being drawn into conflicts, in which their own interests were not seriously engaged, and from which there was no easy escape. In the United States, the Clinton administration led the way by setting new conditions under which the US would be prepared to contribute to multilateral peace-keeping operations – not only would American troops only serve under US command, but they would only engage in operations where time limits could be set in advance and an exit strategy established at the outset.[2]

The realization that civil conflicts could not be resolved on the basis of humanitarian intervention, in the absence of a prior political settlement, had disastrous consequences in Rwanda. When, in April 1994, the Hutu-dominated government embarked upon a systematic genocide of ethnic Tutsi and moderate Hutu, the UN peace-keeping force was scaled down to a point where it could not hope to stem the killing. Moreover, the nineteen countries that had promised troops for a traditional peace-keeping operation, to oversee the implementation of the Arusha Accords, withdrew their offer once it was clear that the agreement was dead and that the conflict had been intensified.[3]

In these circumstances it was perhaps not surprising that the Security Council deliberately refrained from identifying the Rwandan crisis as genocide. To have called the slaughter by its proper name would have made it difficult to avoid intervention. But to do what? In this case the allocation of blame was relatively straightforward, but since the guilty government in Kigali could plausibly claim to represent around 85 per cent of the population, it was unclear on what basis a new order could be constructed, so long as Rwandan society remained divided along ethnic lines. Operation Turquoise, the French-led task force that was eventually sent into the country under a Chapter VII mandate, may have helped to stop the slaughter. But France was so identified with the regime that had initiated the genocide that its failure to separate ordinary refugees from their military and political leaders was – rightly or wrongly – widely regarded as politically motivated.

The failure to take effective action to stop the Rwandan genocide, let alone to forestall it, coincided with the decision of the Security Council to authorize the use of force to restore to power the elected, but subsequently deposed, Haitian President. In taking this decision, the Council referred specifically to 'the significant further deterioration of the humanitarian situation in Haiti, in particular the continuing escalation by the illegal *de facto regime* of systematic violations of civil liberties'.[4] For the first time, force was used by the United Nations to change the government of a member-state. In this sense, a precedent has been set, and the principle of sovereignty interpreted as effective control, on which the society of states had previously operated, was called into question. But it was nonetheless the American interest in stemming the flood of Haitian refugees to the United States, rather than humanitarianism, that finally drove the operation forward.

The answer to the question posed at the beginning of this chapter seems clear. Humanitarian considerations have greater political salience than during the Cold War, but they are insufficient to compel the international community to act in the absence of other more specific strategic or economic motives. Until the Kosovo crisis erupted in 1999 the decline of Security Council activism seemed to confirm the view that the constitutional order of society had not been fundamentally modified. After the Cold War, Western governments took the lead in promoting human rights and democratic values, but their willingness to intervene in the domestic affairs of states whose governments transgressed these norms remained highly selective, particularly where their own interests were not directly involved.

At first sight, this conclusion seems to be reinforced rather than undermined by the international reaction to the Kosovo and East Timor crises. In Kosovo, not only was it impossible to act through the Security Council because of the opposition of Russia and China to NATO's campaign, but the intervention was motivated at least as

much by the need to maintain the organization's credibility and relevance as by humanitarian objectives. Moreover, in bringing the operation to a successful conclusion,
it proved necessary to involve the Russians, whose
interests had been discounted at the outset. In East
Timor, the Western powers returned to the Security
Council and arguably did something to restore its battered
reputation. The jury is also still out on this claim: not only
were the Chinese deeply suspicious of their motives but
by accepting Indonesia's conditions for the conduct of a
plebiscite – namely that the Indonesian military should
stay in charge of security – they acted expediently but
irresponsibly. It was well known that the military were
opposed to giving up the territory and were training local
militias to resist any transfer of power to the nationalists.
By the time a peace-keeping force was set up, these
Indonesian-backed militias had wreaked havoc in an effort
to cow the population into submission. Nonetheless the
scale of the Kosovo operation and the way it was finally
resolved, to be followed almost immediately by the crisis
in East Timor, inevitably reopened the question of the
place of humanitarian intervention in international society
and the current understanding of its core principle of
sovereignty. To conclude this review, let us reconsider
these questions under two heads – the legality of humanitarian intervention and its feasibility.

Let us start with the law. The Kosovo crisis exposed
the sharp conflict between those who view international
society within a legalist paradigm and those who insist on
the primacy of politics. This dispute is not about the
importance of the rule of law to international society, but
about whether it is to be the servant or master of the
state.

During the 1990s, the Security Council adopted a series
of resolutions sanctioning the use of force in support of

humanitarian objectives – in Iraq, Bosnia-Herzegovina, Somalia, Rwanda and Albania. However, as Catherine Guichard has pointed out, 'the combined right of victims to assistance and the right of the Security Council to authorise humanitarian intervention with military means do not amount to a right of humanitarian intervention by states individually or collectively.'[5] The Security Council was able to pass these resolutions because its permanent members were in agreement – and even when China disagreed, it refrained from backing its dissent with a veto – and because in each case the Council ruled that the situation constituted a threat to international peace and security. Neither of these conditions obtained in Kosovo, with the result that the continuing dependence of international law on the competitive political interests of the great powers was made abundantly clear.

Faced with this situation, international lawyers have adopted one of three positions. Some have stuck to the letter of the Charter, arguing that NATO action was illegal and that, regardless of the merits of the ethical argument in this particular case, 'if it is accepted that a state or group of states can unilaterally decide to intervene . . . The door will have been opened to all sorts of subjective claims as to when interventions are justified and when they are not.'[6] Guichard suggested that the Security Council itself should be reformed by 'increasing the representation of Asia, Africa and Latin America, and replacing the right of veto by a system of qualified majority voting'. Such reforms would widen the political basis on which Security Council resolutions depend, and complicate the political bargaining which underlies them. But they would not in themselves subordinate politics to the law. Reaching a consensus would face similar practical difficulties, as would redrafting the Charter to provide for explicit criteria for humanitarian intervention. Whether the end result would justify the requisite investment of time and effort is doubtful.

Finally, there are those who argue that the legal basis of NATO's action is the doctrine of representation which has underpinned the states-system since 1945. Marc Weller argues plausibly that humanitarian action is justified 'where a government or effective authority actively exterminates its populace, or where it denies to it that which is necessary for its survival, or where it forcibly displaces it'.[7] In these circumstances, the government cannot conceivably claim to be the exclusive international representative of that very population. Weller attempts to set restrictive criteria which must be met before a legal dissociation of government and population can be triggered, and suggests that in Kosovo the 12–3 defeat of the Russian draft resolution in the Security Council provides evidence that they had been met. The 98 per cent vote in favour of independence in East Timor presumably provides even more compelling evidence.

Time will tell if international society is, in fact, evolving constitutionally along the lines suggested by this theory. From a political perspective, however, it faces two problems. The first is establishing the criteria, ahead of time, so that they are seen to be more than an *ex-post facto* ratification of a successful plea for intervention. More seriously, even if what Weller calls a fundamental dissociation is accepted as a legitimate trigger, whether or not the theory takes hold will depend crucially on the practical outcome of specific interventions. The law will not stand up if these turn out to have perverse effects.

Turning from the law to the politics, we might start by observing that NATO's action in Kosovo avoided two contradictions in which earlier interventions were mired. The first was the contradiction between ends and means; the second between peace-keeping and enforcement. These contradictions are related. Throughout the early post-Cold War period, the Security Council exhibited a disturbing tendency to will the end but not the means. This tendency arose primarily as a result of uncertainty about the role of peace-keeping forces in civil conflicts. In Kosovo, NATO made it clear from the outset that it was prepared to commit whatever level of air power proved necessary to force President Milosovic to withdraw Yugoslav forces from the province. Since this was the objective, the problem of impartiality did not arise.

At a deeper level, however, it is not clear that these contradictions have been overcome. Apart from the question of legality, most critics of the NATO operation commented on the reluctance of the intervening states – above all the United States – to commit land forces. Their determination to fight a risk-free clean war (at least from their own point of view) revealed a weak point in the democratic armoury. It has been in large part Western public opinion, orchestrated through the media and the NGOs, that has demanded international action in response to humanitarian disasters around the world. At the same time democratic politicians have been understandably wary of putting their own citizens at risk in conflicts that do not directly concern them.

It is arguable that Milosovic would have been prepared to back down sooner had it been made clear to him at the outset, rather than two months into the operation, that NATO would, if necessary, deploy its superior force on land as well as in the air. That they did not do so can perhaps be explained by the difficulty in maintaining solidarity in an alliance, some of whose members would have refused to take part in a land war. On the other hand, since military opinion did not favour an unsupported air war, NATO's political leaders must accept responsibility for the very high levels of damage inflicted on Yugoslavia in pursuit of their goals.

Peace enforcement raises the question of ultimate as well as immediate responsibility. The protection of the victims of persecution and the relief of suffering can be viewed as ends in themselves at the point of intervention. Over the long term, however, it becomes necessary to reconstruct society in ways that will insure against a recurrence of the initial disaster. How is this to be done?

A model of a kind is available. In Cambodia – and to some extent during the transfer of power in Namibia – the UN assumed many of the functions of the civil administration. In both cases it also organized and oversaw the first democratic elections. Then, under the terms of the agreement which had been drawn up prior to its involvement, the UN withdrew. Unfortunately, the model is not well adapted to situations in which the state itself has failed or where – as in Kosovo – the peace that has been enforced requires the dismantling of the previous authority on the grounds that it shares responsibility for the humanitarian disaster.

During the period of Security Council activism after the Cold War, there was talk of reviving the concept of a UN Trusteeship, in order to provide an impartial, stable and accountable administration, in countries that would require an extended period of reconstruction. Intellectually appealing as it was, this idea failed to win any backers amongst governments. The major powers were reluctant to enter into commitments which promised to be both open ended and expensive, and were likely to be criticized for reintroducing imperialism by the back door.

Once the immediate situation has been addressed, however, it is difficult to avoid the conclusion that the logic of humanitarian intervention is imperial. How else is a broken society to be rebuilt? In 1945, the victorious allies demanded unconditional surrender of the German and Japanese governments, precisely because they believed that the only way to avoid history repeating itself was to reconstruct society comprehensively. In these cases, the vital interests of the Western powers were so deeply involved in the outcome that there was no temptation to seek a quick fix and then withdraw. It may be that events will force them to do much the same in Bosnia and Kosovo. In contrast to the Second World War, which was understood to be a fight to the finish from the start, in post-Cold War interventions the international community has involved itself on the understanding that its liability is strictly limited.

In a world without empire, limited liability is probably unavoidable, but in the context of post-war reconstruction it has obvious disadvantages. The overseas empires of the European powers were hardly established to protect the human rights of colonial subjects; but they did inadvertently create professional administrations, staffed by men and women who spoke the languages and understood the culture of the societies they ruled. When the United Nations is brought in to deal with a humanitarian crisis, it has necessarily to employ people on short-term contracts, few of whom will have equivalent expertise. In both Cambodia and Somalia, a lack of local knowledge allowed ambitious and ruthless leaders to exploit the UN for their own purposes. It is not immediately obvious that the organization will be able to avoid this problem in Kosovo, where under Security Council Resolution 1244 an international civil administration has been set up, backed by the NATO-led force of over 50,000.

Two separate problems arise from attempts to establish disinterested administration in countries that have been traumatized by civil conflict. The first concerns the appropriate agency; the second the nature of its mission. The rate at which humanitarian crises followed one another after the Cold War meant that the UN was unable to mobilize the necessary resources, acting on its own. The concept of a 'coalition of the willing', authorized by the UN, was fashioned at the time of the Gulf War and quickly established itself as a standard response to humanitarian crises. After the reverses in Somalia and Rwanda, however, the Western powers were reluctant to involve themselves deeply in conflicts far removed from their own vital interests.

The practical problem was how to avoid being drawn into such conflicts, whenever they captured the world's headlines, and, however briefly, succeeded in mobilizing public opinion. The action of ECOWAS, in mounting a peace-keeping operation in Liberia, initially without the authorization of the Security Council, was seized on as a model for the future. Local powers, supported if necessary with training and technical assistance from the West, should assume primary responsibility for maintaining order and justice within their own region. It could be plausibly argued that if one of the major obstacles to having effective intervention is the absence of knowledge about local conditions, this is more likely to be overcome on a regional level, where normal business and diplomacy create networks across international borders, than universally. Chapter VIII of the Charter had envisaged regional organizations acting in support of the world body. At the start of the twenty-first century, it seems more likely that, in future, the order will be reversed.

An analysis of this kind can be invoked to justify NATO's selectivity in concentrating on Kosovo, and ignoring many other crises, where the criminal activities of the authorities and their oppression of the population is comparable. Serbian policies in Kosovo, on this view, as earlier in Bosnia, threatened the stability, welfare and values of European states, in a way that was not true of Sierra Leone or Myanmar. Similarly, Australia, which led the UN-sponsored peace-keeping operation in East Timor, has both strategic and economic interests in the stability of the Indonesian archipelago. It is true that the wrongs to be righted are universal, but only those in the immediate neighbourhood have both the interest and ability to right them.

There is some force in this argument. It is, after all, the immediate region which feels the first shock of a humanitarian disaster, in the form of refugee flows, and the social and economic problems that they generate. The asylum system was not designed for the mass migrations that result from ethnic cleansing and inter-communal violence. It is not unreasonable, therefore, for the countries most immediately affected by a crisis to accept primary responsibility for orchestrating the international response to it.

Unfortunately, it is also the governments most willing to act that are most likely to have their own political agendas (and clients) in the target state. For much of the time that ECOWAS was involved in Liberia, ECOMOG's work was undermined by the fact that several of its member-states were backing rival factions in the conflict. And when a peace deal was finally negotiated, it was on the basis of a power-sharing agreement between the major warlords, who had previously been accused of devastating the country. Local knowledge, on which ECOMOG could draw, was certainly a crucial element in the process that transformed Charles Taylor from a hunted warlord to an elected president. However, it clearly required a subordination of humanitarian to political and strategic considerations. By opting for a UN-sponsored administration in Kosovo, the intention is presumably to avoid a similar trade-off. Whether this is feasible remains to be seen, but the omens are not favourable.

The reason is partly a consequence of the local culture, but more fundamentally of an unresolved conceptual problem to which regionalization provides no answer. As William Hagen has argued, the analogy between Serbian ethnic cleansing and Nazi genocide against the Jews is misleading: 'Balkan ethnic cleansing does not require mass extermination but rather mass removal, which can be hastened along by displays of murderous violence drawn from the repertory of revenge killings and blood feuds.'[8] This is not to explain the violent politics of former Yugoslavia in terms of ancient hatreds, merely to suggest that the task of any new administration will be greatly complicated by having to operate in an environment where 'the ethic of blood revenge, binding individual members of extended families', has been 'grafted onto ethnic nationalism'.

Just how complicated the task will be was evident from the tension that erupted in August 1999 between NATO and UNHCR. NATO's war had been waged to prevent the ethnic cleansing of Kosovo Albanians, not to facilitate Albanian cleansing of the Serbian minority – hence the importance NATO commanders quite rightly attached to its forces being seen to be impartial. Nonetheless, they were powerless to prevent a spate of revenge killings, which predictably led to a rapid outward migration of the Serb minority. This was aided on the ground by UNHCR, which, in the face of individual atrocities, understandably felt that its humanitarian mission would allow it to do no less. It is difficult to see how in this case two rights could fail to add up to a wrong. From the perspective of humanitarian intervention, the danger is that NATO will have created a land that the KLA – a movement which is a mirror-image of its Serbian enemy – will inherit.

Epilogue

What general conclusions flow from this examination of international relations at the start of the new Millennium?

Perhaps the most important is its emphasis on continuity rather than change. In a world where the rate of technological change appears to advance at an exponential rate, and that has so recently witnessed the disintegration of communism as an ideological and political movement, this claim may seem quixotic. But there is, I submit, little evidence that the fundamental issues of international relations – and they are mainly normative issues – have changed at the same rate, or are likely to do so in the future. This is the justification for the deliberately old-fashioned approach that I have adopted to examine the major challenges to international order that have arisen over the past ten years. The purpose of political analysis, in my view, should not be 'to spot the ball', a doomed but fashionable exercise of trying to second-guess the future. The aim should be more modest, but also more important, namely to construct a framework within which these challenges can be debated intelligibly, that is by citizens and not merely academic experts.

The framework that I have adopted describes the context of international relations in terms of a set of institutions – law, diplomacy, the balance of power etc. – and principles. Some of these – sovereignty, territorial integrity, and non-intervention – have been around since the beginning of the modern states-system. Others – self-determination, non-discrimination, respect for fundamental human rights etc. – have been added more recently. This framework is itself contested, but it is nonetheless familiar, providing a recognizable and, therefore, useful map of the political landscape.

Those who challenge this view argue that it is anachronistic, mapping a world that has disappeared rather than the one we inhabit. But the problem lies less with the map itself than with how to read it, and therefore how, ultimately, to navigate by it. To take, as an illustration, perhaps the most difficult map-reading problem: do all these institutions and principles have equal weight, or are they arranged in a hierarchy? And if so, is it fixed? Alternatively, is it subject to change, in much the same way as a drovers' road – once a major economic artery – may survive as a short cut or an overgrown path used by ramblers or people taking an evening stroll with their dogs. Has law become the master institution in this way, leaving behind the sovereign state, and more particularly the will of the great powers, whose servant it once was?

The discussion of sovereignty, democracy and intervention in this book has led me, I fear, to a pessimistic conclusion on this score. I noted the emergence of a phenomenon that I called virtual sovereignty, which manifests itself in a tendency to attach legal personality to units that can establish a pre-existing historical title, regardless of governmental or administrative capacity. This development extends beyond the distinction between juridical and empirical sovereignty that Robert Jackson developed,[1] in that it increasingly applies to states generally – or at least to a great many of them – and not merely to ex-colonies. But virtual sovereignty is merely one manifestation of a tendency towards virtual liberalism generally. The evidence that we have already encountered comes from many directions – the willingness of the Security Council to will the end rather than the means, the attempt to internationalize democratic values without paying serious attention to social and political conditions, the use of law to pursue only minor tyrants in the name of an allegedly universal prohibition against tyranny, the refusal to accept the imperial logic of humanitarian intervention, and so on.

Originally, as we have seen, international society was conceived as a self-help system. It was not a liberal system – indeed in many respects it was positively illiberal – but while many crimes and inhumanities were concealed behind the self-help formula, it had the advantage, at least, of tying action to responsibility. As a consequence, it established a context in which moral evaluation of politics was not only possible, it was unavoidable. State authorities, which were assumed to act in their own interest, were held to account by the populations they presumed to govern. Accountability was either through the ballot box, or, in its absence, eventually by rebellion. Internationally co-ordinated action was rare, and depended on the consent of the parties.

By contrast, who would have been held responsible had the indictment of General Pinochet sparked off an anti-democratic backlash in Chile? And did the fact that East Timor had been illegally annexed by Indonesia – in defiance of the conventional interpretation of national self-determination as decolonization – justify accepting a timetable for a referendum that left the UN dependent on the Indonesian military, not only the most powerful of that country's institutions, but one which was known to be deeply opposed to surrendering the territory? It would not be difficult to find other examples.

Behind these examples lies a more fundamental question: can international society be improved? The tension between the idea of an international society of states bound together by a law of coexistence, and one in which that society is understood as a way station *en route* to a genuine community of humankind, is not new. What is new is that, in the aftermath of the Cold War, it is no longer possible to avoid confronting the meaning of progress in relation to international relations.

During the Cold War, it was possible to postpone this confrontation by conceding that while both communism and liberal capitalism rested on competing teleologies, the strategic stalemate between the powers arraigned on each side of the ideological divide, ensured that, international politics would conform to a power political model, under which gains and losses were ultimately viewed as absolute. The problem is not merely that the end of the Cold War inevitably puts the surviving teleology under the microscope, but also that the power political model, which was reluctantly accepted even by most liberals during it, is no longer available, globally, as a framework for normative debate.

The existence of a single superpower creates the danger of unrestrained global action, and, therefore, on one reading of the historical record, suggests that sooner or later a new countervailing alliance will arise to prevent the consolidation of a world empire. But one does not have to accept a fully-fledged version of the globalization thesis, in which the state withers away in the face of market pressures, to judge that this mode of argument may be anachronistic. The Cold War accommodation between ideological and power political struggle depended on both elements. A future power political struggle, which is not supported by any underlying rationale, is not unimaginable, but seems unlikely.

So we have to re-examine the idea of progress in relation to international society. The first and most obvious point is to note that the original framework was laid out without reference to progressive ideas. Indeed, it was laid out as a way of putting an end to the carnage caused by the attempt to monopolize the route in this world, to salvation in the next. Only with the transfer of sovereignty from the princes to the people after 1918, was the idea of salvation – now in secular form – reintroduced as a central preoccupation of international relations. Since then, it has been reinforced twice – after 1945 by the introduction of the idea that people everywhere have a right to economic welfare and after 1989 by the renewed emphasis on fundamental human rights generally and the right to democratic governance in particular. A case can be made that liberal economic management has added at the margin to global welfare, but after the holocaust, the Gulag, and the more recent wave of ethnic and communal conflicts and genocides, it is difficult to claim that the reintroduction of global conviction politics has led to greater world-wide justice.

I do not wish to imply that we can put the clock back, let alone that we should aspire to do so. On the contrary, it seems to me that we are stuck with the idea of progress, even though increasingly we are unsure about what it means. The modern world cannot easily escape its historical mode of thought; it follows the arrow of time wherever it leads and despite its problematic and, under some circumstances, ominous implications for international relations. We are stuck with the idea of progress because it is the coin of democratic politics. It provides its underlying ethic, as tragedy provided it when the fate of peoples was subsumed in the fate of their leaders, whose humanity had to play second fiddle to their role. Even conservatives acknowledge the progressive idiom of modern politics. In

Lampedusa's magnificent novel *The Leopard*, the young Tancredi understands this logic, as does the old Duke, who nonetheless rejects it. Tancredi pleads unsuccessfully with him to become a senator in the newly unified Italy. In words that foreshadow the world of virtual liberalism, he says that if things are to stay the same, they must change. Within democratic countries, it is impossible to conceive of politics without competition between alternative visions of the future. By now, in the West, it is no longer just the conservatives who treat the rival manifestos advanced in the name of liberty and equality with the irony they deserve. We all do it. But only up to a point: without them we could not be got to the polls.

At the international level, we lack the thick social structure, that is the rituals of everyday life, to sustain us when the politicians fail to deliver. So it is more difficult to create an ironic safety valve, even though arguably one is even more necessary. What is at issue, after all, is the constitution of international society itself. If that constitution allows Russia to drive Chechen civilians from their homes with impunity, while it permits – and on one reading of the law encourages – NATO to drive the Serbs from Kosovo, do not power and interest still carry all before them? So runs the radical progressive critique of our present international order. On this view international norms are, as they always have been, merely a veneer over the ambitions of ruthless men.

At this stage in the argument, it is tempting to seek refuge in the coexistence of the three traditions for the interpretation of international society that we encountered in part I of this book. Only the revolutionaries – the theorists will tell us – adopt a fundamentalist position that equates progress with the wholesale transformation of the states-system. Realists do not need to worry since they have always regarded moral considerations as irrelevant to

foreign policy. Liberal rationalists believe that international society can be improved, but not by force. Historically, and regrettably, they have always been disposed
to adopt a literal definition of force. Predictably, in the
Chechen crisis, there were frequent calls for economic
sanctions, by those who accepted that the international
community neither could, nor should, intervene militarily.

None of these traditional responses seems convincing,
at least if presented in their essentialist form. The revolutionary view of the future is the least plausible. Not
merely has the collectivist vision of world society failed,
but the various neo-Kantian versions of the argument,
which allow for an evolution of self-consciousness to a
point where it transcends particular interests, seem
increasingly heroic. Rationalist responses – particularly
those that seek to bring about a better future by a combination of institutional engineering and economic pressure
– are psychologically unconvincing and often self-delud-
ing. Indeed, deracinated rationalism must bear much of
the responsibility for the emergence of virtual liberalism.
Had Western governments paid more attention to the
ancestor of economic sanctions, namely siege warfare,
they might have been less inclined to believe in their utility
as an instrument of democratization in Iraq, Haiti or
Serbia. The objective of a siege was, after all, to starve the
occupants of a castle or inhabitants of a city into submission. And it was surely rationalism on stilts which
persuaded the Security Council that Indonesian-trained
militia would melt into the background in the face of a
UN-administered plebiscite.

We return finally, therefore, to realism. Realism considered as amoralism, as power politics unmediated even
by prudence, is the most implausible response of all. But
the idea of morality as an 'add-on' has always been a
straw man. It is no accident that David Hume, Adam

Smith and the other savants of the Scottish Enlightenment, in seeking to ground rationalism in empirical reality,
devoted so much time to analysing moral reasoning. No
one who has been involved in decisions that are weighed
down with fateful consequences can afford to ignore the
calculation of risks and probabilities. From this point of
view, prudence is a virtue. Without prudence all visions of
the future degenerate into mere utopia, with all its attend-
ant dangers.

Realism, viewed as I am suggesting it should be,
involves a moral perspective, which we ignore at our peril.
It should be viewed, not simply as power politics but as
the position that requires human beings to take responsibility for their actions, and to acknowledge that these will
have unintended as well as predictable consequences. It
remains true that realism sits more easily with a tragic
than with a progressive view of the human condition. And
it is because a secular and democratic civilization – or
rather one in which public standards are set by democratic
criteria – that we have such difficulty in fashioning a
morally relevant form of realism.

It is beyond the scope of this short book to suggest how
this should be done. That it is the major challenge for our
time, however, is not seriously in doubt. If the scientists
are to be believed – and they too masquerade in many
ideological colours – the planet is now in potentially
terminal crisis. It is as dangerous to assume that those
who predict devastating consequences as a result of global
warming over the next fifty years are being hysterical, as it
is to assume that the global market will solve all our
problems. If the pessimists are right, the problems of
entrenching human rights and democratic governance,
that I have discussed here, will pale into insignificance.
We cannot know which of these alternatives – or indeed
what other possibility – will come true. In the meantime,

we have no realistic alternative than to approach the future with caution, but also with hope. Democratic politics cannot appropriate the tragic idiom, even though contemporary governments may be facing a tragedy of far greater magnitude than their aristocratic forebears could have envisaged. The short run will continue to dominate politics; that is their nature. But we know that the pace of modern life has vastly quickened during our lifetime and continues to do so. Consequently, what counts as the short run, that is, the period during which we can legitimately claim that those who take decisions must also accept responsibility for them, has lengthened. We have not yet found a way of aligning our politics with this reality. The way forward is not to argue that Hume's insistence that our morals should not outstrip our experience is out of date, but to bring our experience to bear on the moral dilemmas that now confront us.

Notes

Prologue

1 Samuel P. Huntingdon, *The Clash of Civilizations and the Remaking of the World Order* (New York, Simon and Schuster, 1996).

Chapter 1   Origins and Stucture

1 Martin Wight identified nine distinct meanings. See 'The Balance of Power', in Herbert Butterfield and Martin Wight (eds), *Diplomatic Investigations* (London, George Allen and Unwin,1966) pp. 149–75.
2 See Hedley Bull, *The Anarchical Society: A Study of Order in World Politics*, (London, Macmillan, 1977), pp. 23–52; and Martin Wight, *International Theory: The Three Traditions*, ed. Gabriele Wight and Brian Porter (Leicester, Leicester University Press for the RIIA, 1991), pp. 7–24.
3 See, for example, J. Scott Keltie, *The Partition of Africa* (London 1895), and James Lorrimer, *The Institutes of the Law of Nations* (Edinburgh, 1883), vol. 1.

Chapter 2　The Modernization of International Society

1　Wight, *International Theory*, pp. 49–50.
2　Ibid.

Chapter 3　A New Solidarism?

1　See Ernest Gellner, *Legitimation of Belief* (Cambridge University Press, 1974), pp. 1–23.
2　David Hume, *A Treatise on Human Nature*, vol. 2, section XI, 'Of the law of Nations', (Everyman edition, London, J. M. Dent) p. 265.
3　Ibid.

Chapter 4　Nationalism

1　Boutros Boutros-Ghali, *Agenda for Peace*, paragraphs 17 and 18. For text see A. Roberts and B. Kingsbury (eds), *United Nations, Divided World: The UN's Roles in International Relations*, 2nd edn (Oxford, Clarendon Press, 1993), Appendix A, pp. 468–98.
2　J. S. Mill, *Representative Government*, ch. 16, numerous editions.
3　G. W. F. Hegel, *Philosophy of Right*, tr. T. M. Knox (Oxford, Oxford University Press, 1979), Part 3: Ethical Life, (iii) The State, (c) World History. 'Civilised Nations [are justified] in regarding and treating as barbarians those who lag behind them in institutions which are the essential moments of the State. Thus a pastoral people may treat hunters as barbarians and both of these are barbarians from the point of view of agriculturalists etc. The civilised nation is conscious that the rights of barbarians are unequal to its own and treats their autonomy as only a formality.

4   W. I. Jennings, *The Approach to Self-Government* (Cambridge, Cambridge University Press, 1956), p. 56.
5   See A. D. Smith, 'Ethnie and Nation in the Modern World', *Millennium, Journal of International Studies*, 14/2 (summer 1985), pp. 127–42.
6   Walker Connor, 'When is a Nation', *Ethnic and Racial Studies*, 13 (1990), pp. 82–100.
7   E. Gellner, *Conditions of Liberty: Civil Society and its Rivals* (London, Hamish Hamilton, 1994), p. 113.
8   Ibid., p. 116.
9   B. Anderson, *Imagined Communities: Reflections on the Origins and Spread of Nationalism* (London, Verso, 1983), pp. 50–65.

Chapter 5   Self-determination

1   'Tanzania's Memorandum on Biafra's Case'. For text, see A. H. M. Kirk-Greene (ed.), *Crisis and Conflict in Nigeria: A Documentary Sourcebook*, vol. 2, *July 1967–January 1970* (Oxford, Oxford University Press, 1971), pp. 429–39.
2   M. Glenny, *The Fall of Yugoslavia* (Harmondsworth, Penguin, 1992), p. 179.
3   See B. O'Leary, 'Insufficiently Liberal and Insufficiently Nationalist', in 'Symposium on David Miller's *On Nationality*', *Nations and Nationalism*, 2 (1996), p. 450 n. 4.
4   H. Beran, *The Consent Theory of Political Obligation* (London, Croom Helm, 1987), pp. 39–42.

Chapter 6   Reappraisal

1   See Sally Healey, 'The Changing Idiom of Self-determination in the Horn of Africa', in I. M. Lewis (ed.) *Nationalism and Self-Determination in the Horn of Africa* (London, Ithaca Press, 1983), pp. 101–3.
2   For an account of the UN negotiations on the Italian colonies, see P. Calvocoressi, *Survey of International Affairs,*

1947–1948 and 1949–1950, (Oxford, Oxford University Press for RIIA), pp. 121–3 and 539–55.

3   Department of Justice, Canada, backgrounder, 27 February 1997.

4   Robert Jackson, *Quasi-states: Sovereignty, International Relations and the Third World* (Cambridge, Cambridge University Press,1990), pp. 18–21.

5   F. List, *The National System of Political Economy* (1841; tr. Sampson S. Lloyd, New York, Longmans Green, 1904).

6   A. S. Milwood, with the assistance of G. Brennan and F. Romero, *The European Rescue of the Nation State* (London, Routledge,1992).

Chapter 7   Historical Antecedents and Cultural Preconditions

1   Boutros Boutros-Ghali, *Agenda for Peace: Preventive Diplomacy, Peacemaking and Peace-keeping*, Report of the Secretary-General pursuant to the statement adopted by the Summit Meeting of the Security Council on 31 January 1992 (New York, United Nations, 1992), para. 19.

2   See James Mayall, 'Democratizing the Commonwealth', *International Affairs*, 74/2, (April 1998).

3   Anthony Lake, 'From Containment to Enlargement', *Dispatch*, 4/39, (1993).

4   George F. Kennan, *The Cloud of Danger: Some Current Problems of American Foreign Policy* (London, Hutchinson, 1977), pp. 41–6.

5   See Bull, *The Anarchical Society*, part 2, pp. 101–232.

6   James Mayall, *Nationalism and International Society* (Cambridge, Cambridge University Press, 1990), pp. 25–6.

7   A. H. Hansen, 'Power Shifts and Regional Balances', in Paul Streeton and Michael Lipton (eds), *The Crisis of Indian Planning* (Oxford, Oxford University Press for the RIIA, 1968), p. 43.

8   Quoted in Stephen E. Ambrose, *Undaunted Courage* (New York, Touchstone, Simon and Schuster, 1996), pp. 188–9.

9   Ernest Gellner, *Conditions of Liberty, Civil Society and its Rivals* (London, Hamish Hamilton, 1994), p. 87.

10   Ibid., p. 188.

Chapter 8   International Law and the Instruments of Foreign Policy

1   James Crawford, *Democracy in International Law*, Inaugural Lecture, 5 March 1993 (Cambridge, Cambridge University Press, 1994), pp. 8–10.

2   House of Lords, Session 1998–9, *Judgement – Regina v. Bartle and the Commissioner of Police for the Metropolis and others Ex Parte Pinochet, Regina v. Evans and Another and the Commissioner of Police for the Metropolis and Others Ex Parte Pinochet (On Appeal from a Divisional Court of the Queen's Bench Division)*.

3   *The Times*, 29 March 1999, p. 20.

4   United Nations General Assembly, *Support by the United Nations System of the Efforts of Governments to Promote and Consolidate New or Restored Democracies*, A/53/554, 29 October 1998.

5   Henrik Ibsen, *An Enemy of the People*, 1883, Act IV. 'The majority has the might – more's the pity – but it hasn't right . . . the minority is always right.'

6   'Local Interference with Foreign Policy', *Boston Globe*, 9 November 1998.

Chapter 9   Pluralism and Solidarism Revisited

1   J. Huizinga, *Homo Ludens: A Study of the Play Element in Culture* (London, Temple Smith, 1970), pp. 110–26.

2   F. Gilbert, 'The New Diplomacy of the Eighteenth Century', *World Politics*, 4 (1951), pp. 1–38.

3   See D. Baldwin and H. Milner (eds), *East–West Trade and*

the Atlantic Alliance (New York, St Martin's Press, 1990), chapters 4 and 7.

4 International Task Force on the Enforcement of UN Security Council Resolutions, *Words to Deeds: Strengthening the UN's Enforcement Capabilities, Final Report* (United Nations Association of the United States of America, 1997).

5 See David Malone, *Decision-Taking in the UN Security Council, 1990–1996: The Case of Haiti* (Oxford, Oxford University Press, 1998).

6 J. Jackson-Preece, 'National Minority Rights v. State Sovereignty in Europe: Changing Norms in International Relations?', *Nations and Nationalism*, 3 (1997), pp. 347–9.

7 Article 27 stipulates that 'in those states in which ethnic, religious or linguistic minorities exist, persons belonging to such minorities shall not be denied the right, in community with other members of their group, to enjoy their own culture, to profess and practice their own religion, or to use their own language.'

8 Quoted in R. L. Barsh, 'Indigenous Peoples in the 1990s: From Object to Subject of International Law', *Harvard Human Rights Journal*, 7 (1994), pp. 36–46.

9 UN Doc. E/CN.4/Sub.2/1993/3/26 (1993).

Chapter 10   Intervention in Liberal International Theory

1 Quoted in Paul Rogers, 'Lessons to Learn', *World Today*, 55/8–9 (August/September 1999), pp. 4–6.

2 For the full list, see Marack Goulding, 'The United Nations and Conflict in Africa since the Cold War', *African Affairs*, 98/391 (April 1999), table I, p. 158.

3 For a range of assessments, see Mats Berdal, *Whither UN Peacekeeping*, Adelphi Paper 281 (London, Brasseys for IISS, 1993); Adam Roberts, *Humanitarian Action in War*, Adelphi Paper 305 (London, Brasseys for IISS, 1996); James Mayall (ed.), *The New Interventionism: UN Experience*

in Cambodia, Former Yugoslavia and Somalia (Cambridge, Cambridge University Press, 1996).

Chapter 11   Humanitarian Intervention in the 1990s

1 See Edward Luttwak, 'Give War a Chance', *Foreign Affairs*, 78/4, (July/August 1999), pp. 36–44.
2 Mayall (ed.), *The New Interventionism*, p. 118 n. 34.
3 Goulding, 'The United Nations and Conflict in Africa since the Cold War', p. 163.
4 Security Council Resolution 940, 31 July 1994.
5 Catherine Guichard, 'International Law and the War in Kosovo', *Survival*, 41/2, (summer 1999), pp. 19–34.
6 Michael Byers, 'Kosovo: An Illegal Operation', *Counsel* (August 1999), pp. 16–18.
7 Marc Weller, 'Armed Samaritans', *Counsel* (August 1999), pp. 20–2.
8 William Hagen, 'The Balkans' Lethal Nationalisms', *Foreign Affairs*, 78/4, (July/August 1999), pp. 52–64.

Epilogue

1 R. Jackson, *Quasi-states: Sovereignty, International Relations and the Third World* (Cambridge, Cambridge University Press, 1990).

Index

Agenda for Peace, 40, 60, 81, 108
Aid, 100
Albania, 125, 141
Amin, President Idi Amin, 132
Anderson, Benedict, 48
Armenia, 67
Azerbaijan, 67

Balance of power, 11–12
Bangladesh, 39, 55
Beran, Harry, 60, 61
Bhutan, 76
Biafra, 55
Bosnia, 61, 69, 125, 141, 145
    NATO forces in, 70
Boutros Boutros-Ghali, 40, 60, 81, 82, 108

Caesar, Julius, 1
Cambodia, 100, 132, 134, 144, 145
Canada, and Quebec, 62, 73–4
Carter, President Jimmy, 82

Chad, 67
Chechenya, 154–5
China, 56, 100, 124
    and human rights, 106
Christianity, 2, 5
    Christian era, 11
    United Christendom, idea of, 12
Clinton, President Bill, 81
Commonwealth, 81, 101, 109, 110, 119
Communism, collapse of, 57, 134, 149
Community of Mankind, 16, 27
Council of Europe, 57, 81, 107, 114
Croatia, 61

Dayton Accords, The, 58, 69–70, 125
    and conventional interpretation of national self-determination, 70
Decolonization, 32, 52, 87

Decolonization (*cont'd*)
  and disintegration of
    USSR, 57, 67
  and territorial adjustment,
    54
De Gaulle, President Charles,
  policy towards Biafra, 55
Democracy
  and cultural diversity, 89
  and international law, 94–5
  and nomadic societies,
    90–1
Diplomacy, 89, 100

East Timor, 71, 139–42, 147
  annexation by Indonesia,
    72
  opposition of Indonesian
    military to plebiscite in,
    140
Economic Community of
  West African States
  (ECOWAS), 98, 146, 147
Economic sanctions, 100–4,
  155
Eritrea
  secession from Ethiopia, 71
  admission to UN and
    OAU, 72
European states-system, 15, 75
  attitude to Oriental powers,
    16
European Union, 57, 77, 78,
  81, 107, 114
  Badinter Commission, 58

Fiji, 100, 119–20

Gandhi, Indira, 1
Gellner, Ernest, 48, 49, 50,
  92
General Agreement on Tariffs
  and Trade (GATT), 22
Genocide Convention, 132,
  133
Goff, Lord, 96
Golan Heights, Israel's
  occupation of, 68
Grotius, Hugo, 27, 128
Guichard, Catherine, 141

Hagen, William, 148
Haiti, 111, 125, 139
Hegel, G.W.F, 44
Hezbullah, 33
Human Rights, 23, 27, 96,
  99, 139
  and minority rights, 41,
    112–15
  Universal Declaration of,
    33, 45, 53, 113, 132
  Vienna Conference on
    (1993), 35, 116
Hume, David, 28, 29, 31, 35,
  155–6
Huntingdon, Samuel, 3

India, 39, 61, 77, 97, 117,
  124, 132
Indigenous peoples' rights,
  115–18
International Bank for
  Reconstruction and
  Development (IBRD), 22
International Monetary Fund
  (IMF), 22

International Society, 11–16, 20, 31, 34, 61, 83–5, 151–3
  admission of Asian and Latin American countries, 20
  and democracy, 82
  and dynasticism, 42
  and pluralism, 84, 88, 111–12
  and sanctions, 103
  and United Nations Organization, 97
  impact of American and French Revolutions on, 42
  precarious foundations of, 26
Iraq, 123, 124, 141
Irish Free State, secession from UK, 73
Irredentism, 54, 113, 115
Islam, 5

Jackson, Robert, 75
Jackson-Preece, Jennifer, 113
Jefferson, President, 90
Jennings, Ivor, 45
Jinnah, Mohammad Ali, 60

Kant, Immanuel, 18, 111
Kennan, George, 82
Kenya, 100
Kosovo, 84, 96, 97, 123, 124, 126, 139–47
  and conventional interpretation of national self-determination, 70

Krajina, 61, 125
Kurds, 32
Kuwait, 123, 124, 135

Lake, Anthony, 81
League of Nations, 112
  mandate system, 19
Lebanon, 67
Lewis, Captain Merriweather, 90
Liberal ideology, 19, 104–5
  thinkers, 6
Liberia, 147
Lincoln, President Abraham, 60, 64
List, F., 77

Marx, Karl, 127
Marxism, 2
Mboya, Tom, 84
Mercantalism, 3, 130
Mill, John Stuart, 44, 63, 113, 130–1
Milosovic, President Slobodan, 58, 84
Minority Rights, 112–15
Mitterrand, President François, 107
Morocco, claims to Mauretania and Western Sahara, 71
Mozambique, 100, 134
Muslim League, 60
Myanmar, 100, 147

Namibia, 134, 144
Nationalism, 44, 85
  and relationship to self-

Nationalism (*cont'd*)
    determination and
        sovereignty, 41, 45
Nations
    and relationship to
        democracy, 64–5
    and reliance on pre-existing
        boundaries, 50–1
    origins of, 45–8
Nehru, Jawaharlal, 88
Ngorno Karabach, Armenian
    occupation of, 68
Nigeria, 100, 110
North Atlantic Treaty
    Organization (NATO),
        58, 70, 84, 96, 97, 98,
        105, 123, 124, 126, 139,
        141, 142, 148
Norway, secession from
    Sweden, 73
Nyerere, President Julius, 55,
    56

Operation Desert Storm, 98,
    123
Operation Turquoise,
    138
Organization of African Unity
    (OAU), 55, 56
    and principle of *uti
        possidetis*, 70
Organization for Security and
    Co-operation in Europe
    (OSCE), 111
Ottoman Empire, 15
    disposal of Levantine
        provinces, 19

Pakistan, 61, 110
Pascal, Blaise, 7
Perpetual Peace, 18; *see also*
    Kant, Immanuel
Pinochet, President Augusto,
    96
Pluralism, 14, 21, 84, 88
Pol Pot, 132
Portugal, 87
Powell, Enoch, 64

Quebec, 62, 73–4

Reagan, President Ronald, 1
Rees-Mogg, William, 96
Renan, A. , 65
Representative Government, 63;
    see also Mill, John Stuart
Robertson, George, 124
Roman Empire, 12
Rousseau, J.-J., 44
Rwanda, 125, 138, 141,
    146
    genocide in, 61, 138

San Marino, 77
Secession, 56, 61, 73, 113,
    115
    arguments against, 60–6
    in Katanga, Biafra and
        Bangladesh, 55
Self- determination, 20, 40,
    42, 45, 56, 57, 59, 84
    conventional interpretation
        of, 41, 52, 67, 69, 71, 73,
        108
    demands by stateless
        groups for, 39

and democratic self-
government, 112,
118–20, 129
and devolution, 78
national, 43
and plebiscites, 45
regressive, 61–2
and relationship to
sovereignty, 41
and secession, 61
Sierra Leone, 110, 147
Singapore, secession from
Malaysia, 73
Slovakia, secession from
Czech republic, 73
Smith, Adam, 127, 156
Solidarism, 14, 21, 26, 85
Somalia, 91, 100, 125, 135–7,
145, 146
irredentist claims of, 71
Somaliland, Republic of,
72
South Africa, 100
Sovereignty, 18, 21, 35, 39,
67, 74
empirical and juridical,
74–5, 76, 150
of individuals, 27
of peoples, 18, 53
popular, 17, 30, 32, 42, 95,
112, 129
and relationship to self-
determination, 41
and territorial integrity, 13,
126
virtual, 76, 150
Sri Lanka, Tamils of North
East, 32

State, The
doctrine of state immunity,
95–6
narrowing of competence,
75

Tanzania, 132
Taylor, President Charles,
147
Territory, sacralization of, 32,
112
Thatcher, Margaret, 107
Thirty Years War, 15; *see also*
Wars of Religion)

Ukraine, 32
United Nations Organization
(UNO), 32, 56, 100,
103, 145
charter of, 19, 45, 53
financial crisis in,
135
General Assembly, 55
and international society,
69, 97, 100
peace-keeping and peace-
building, 134–48
Secretary-General Boutros
Boutros-Ghali, 40, 60,
81, 82, 108
Secretary-General Kofi
Annan, 99
Security Council, 30, 68,
69, 97, 98, 111, 123,
124, 131, 132–3, 141,
143, 144
and sovereignty, 75
Trusteeship Council, 20

United States of America
(USA), 24, 56, 81, 106,
107, 123, 139, 143
   purchase of Alaska and
   Louisiana, 77
USSR (Soviet Union), 24, 32
   borders of successor states,
   58
   disintegration of, 57, 134
Uti possidetis juris, principle of,
68–70

Vattel, E., 27

Wars of Religion, 12, 13
Weller, Marc, 148

Westphalia, Peace of 1648,
11, 15, 19, 127
Wight, Martin, 13, 23
Wilson, President Woodrow,
18, 19, 105
World Trade Organization
(WTO), 33, 101, 104,
127

Yugoslavia, 57, 58, 126,
135–6, 144
   withdrawal from Kosovo,
   58

Zimbabwe, 124